P9-BZI-539

Internet
in an Hour
for Beginners

Don Mayo
Kathy Berkemeyer

Acknowledgements

To my mother and sister for all their love and support, and to my friend Midori for hooking me up with such a great gig!
Don Mayo

Dedicated to the memory of my parents, John and Gert Madden.
Kathy Berkemeyer

Managing Editor	Technical Editors	English Editor	Illustrations	Design and Layout
Jennifer Frew	Monique Peterson	Monique Peterson	Ryan Sather	Elsa Johannesson
	Cathy Vesecky			Midori Nakamura
				Paul Wray

Copyright© 1998 by DDC Publishing, Inc.
Published by DDC Publishing, Inc.
The information contained herein is copyrighted by DDC Publishing, Inc.
All right reserved, including the right to reproduce this book or portions thereof in any form whatsoever. For information, address DDC Publishing, Inc., 275 Madison Avenue, 12th Floor, New York, New York 10016
Internet address: *http://www.ddcpub.com*

ISBN: 1-56243-603-1
Cat. No. HR3
First DDC Publishing, Inc. Printing:
10 9 8 7 6 5 4 3 2
Printed in the United States of America.

Netscape™, Netscape™ Communications logo, Netscape™ Communications Corporation, Netscape™ Communications, Netscape Mail™, and Netscape™ Navigator are all trademarks of Netscape™ Communications Corporation.
Microsoft® and Windows® are registered trademarks of the Microsoft Corporation.
Yahoo!™ and Yahoo™ logo are trademarks of Yahoo!™
LYCOS™, LYCOS™ logo are trademarks of LYCOS™.
AltaVista™ and the AltaVista™ logo are trademarks of AltaVista Technology, Inc.
Digital™ and the Digital™ logo are trademarks of Digital Equipment Corporation.
Excite is a service mark of Excite Inc
Bigfoot and Bigfoot footprint are service marks of Bigfoot Partners L.P.
Four11 is the property of Four11 Corporation.
Internet Address Finder is the property of DoubleClick Inc.
Switchboard™ is a trademark of Banyan Systems Inc.
WhoWhere?™ and the WhoWhere?™ logo are trademarks of WhoWhere? Inc.
Some illustrations in this book and on the DDC Web site have been acquired from Web sites and are used for demonstration and educational purposes only. Online availability of text and images does not imply that they may be reused without the permission of the copyright holder, although the Copyright Act does permit certain unauthorized reuse as fair use under 17 U.S.C. Section 107

All registered trademarks, trademarks, and service marks are the property of their respective companies.

Contents

Contents

Introduction

This Book is Designed for You . . .

if you are new to the Internet or you are not sure what kind of information is available to you online.

The Internet and especially the World Wide Web provide a vast and ever-growing resource where you can find information and entertainment. This book shows you where and how to find the best resources available.

This book has two main sections, Internet Basics and Web Resources.

Internet Basics

In Internet Basics, you can learn how to:

- Use Netscape Navigator to browse the World Wide Web.
- Send and receive e-mail messages with Netscape Messenger.
- Use Internet Explorer to browse the World Wide Web.
- Send and receive e-mail messages with Microsoft Outlook Express.
- Access the Internet using America Online.
- Send and receive e-mail messages with America Online.
- Find information on the Web with search engines.

Web Resources

Web Resources shows you ways you can use the Web to find both practical and fun information.

Web Resources is organized by general categories (such as Online Shopping, Monetary Matters, Arts and Entertainment), then by topics (such as Movie Lovers' Online Resources, Plan and Book Travel Online, and Personal Finances).

Each topic showcases top Web sites that offer excellent information. The Web site listings provide you with the site's URL (Web address) and a brief description of how the site can help you. In many cases an illustration of the Web site is also provided.

Appendices

These Appendices give you additional reference information about the following topics:

Essential Downloads

A listing of Web sites where you can download useful software, much of it available free of charge or for a minimal registration fee.

Timesaving Tools

Use these sites to get quick answers and information.

Emoticons and Abbreviations

Symbols and abbreviations used when communicating electronically.

Netiquette

A guide to using "net etiquette" when communicating and browsing online.

Viruses

An overview of what computer viruses can do to your computer and how to avoid them.

Glossary

A listing of Internet and World Wide Web terminology complete with definitions.

What Do I Need to Use This Book

This book assumes that you have some general knowledge and experience with computers, and that you already know how to perform the following tasks:

- Use a mouse (double-click, etc.).
- Make your way around Microsoft Windows 95.
- Install and run programs.

If you are completely new to computers as well as the World Wide Web, you may want to refer to DDC's **Learning Microsoft Windows 95** or **Learning the Internet**.

This book also assumes that you have access to browser applications such as Microsoft Internet Explorer 4.0, Netscape Navigator 4.0, or America Online.

√ *If you do not currently have these applications, contact your Internet Service Provider for instructions on how to download them. You can also use other browsers or previous versions such as Explorer 3.0 and Navigator 3.0 to browse the Web.*

You must have an Internet connection, either through your school, your office, or an online service such as America Online or CompuServe. How to get connected to the Internet is not covered in this book.

Please read over the following list of "must haves" to ensure that you are ready to be connected to the Internet.

- A computer (with a recommended minimum of 16 MB of RAM) and a modem port.

- A modem (with a recommended minimum speed of 14.4kbps, and suggested speed of 28.8kbps) that is connected to an analog phone line (assuming you are not using a direct Internet connection through a school, corporation, etc.).

- Established access to the Internet through an online service, independent Internet service provider, etc.

- A great deal of patience. The Internet is a fun and exciting place. But getting connected can be frustrating at times. Expect to run into occasional glitches, to get disconnected from time to time, and to experience occasional difficulty in viewing certain Web pages or features. The more up-to-date your equipment and software are, however, the less difficulty you will probably experience.

Internet Cautions

ACCURACY: Be cautious not to believe everything on the Internet. Almost anyone can publish information on the Internet, and since there is no Internet editor or monitor, some information may be false. All information found on the World Wide Web should be checked for accuracy through additional reputable sources.

SECURITY: When sending information over the Internet, be prepared to let the world have access to it. Computer hackers can find ways to access anything that you send to anyone over the Internet, including e-mail. Be cautious when sending confidential information to anyone.

VIRUSES: These small, usually destructive computer programs hide inside of innocent-looking programs. Once a virus is executed, it attaches itself to other programs. When triggered, often by the occurrence of a date or time on the computer's internal clock/calendar, it executes a nuisance or damaging function, such as displaying a message on your screen, corrupting your files, or reformatting your hard disk.

BASICS

Netscape Navigator: 1

◆ About Netscape Navigator ◆ Start Netscape Navigator
◆ The Netscape Screen ◆ Exit Netscape Navigator

About Netscape Navigator

■ Netscape Navigator 4.0 is the Internet browser component of Netscape Communicator, a set of integrated tools for browsing the World Wide Web, finding and downloading information, shopping for and purchasing goods and services, creating Web pages, and communicating with others with e-mail. This chapter focuses on the Netscape Navigator browser. Netscape Messenger, the e-mail component, is covered in Chapters 4-6.

Start Netscape Navigator

To start Netscape Navigator (Windows 95):

• Click the Start button **Start**.

• Click Programs, Netscape Communicator, Netscape Navigator.

OR

• If you have a shortcut to Netscape Communicator on your desktop, double-click it to start Netscape Navigator.

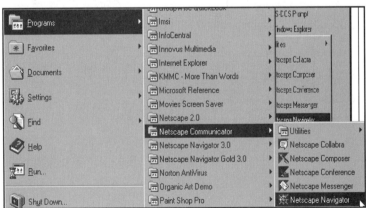

√ *The first time you start Netscape Communicator, the New Profile Setup dialog box appears. Enter information about your e-mail name and service provider in the dialog boxes that appear. If you do not know the information, you can leave it blank until you are ready to fill it in.*

The Netscape Screen

- The Netscape Navigator screen contains features that will be very helpful as you explore the Internet. Some of these features are constant and some change depending on the Web site visited or the task attempted or completed.

  √ *To gain more space on screen, you may want to hide toolbars and the Location line. Go to the View menu and select the desired hide/show options.*

Title bar   Displays the name of the program (Netscape) and the current Web page (Welcome to Netscape). Note the standard Windows minimize, maximize/restore, and close buttons at the right.

Menu bar   Displays menus, which provide drop-down lists of commands for executing Netscape tasks.

Navigation toolbar   Contains buttons for moving between and printing Web pages. The name and icon on each button identify the command for the button. You can access these commands quickly and easily by clicking the mouse on the desired button.

If the toolbar buttons are not visible, open the View menu and click Show Navigation Toolbar.

Location toolbar   Displays the electronic address of the currently displayed Web page in the Location field. You can also type the electronic address of a Web page in the Location field and press Enter to access it. A Web site address is called a Uniform Resource Locator (URL).

If the Location toolbar is not visible, open the View menu and click Show Location Toolbar.

| | The Location toolbar also contains the Bookmarks QuickFile button. Click this button to view a list of sites that you have bookmarked for quick access. (For more information on bookmarks, see "Netscape Navigator: 3" on page 9.) |

The Location button is also located on this toolbar. The word *Netsite* displays if the current Web site uses Netscape software. The word *Location* replaces Netsite if the site does not use Netscape as its primary software.

Personal toolbar — Contains buttons or links that you add to connect to your favorite sites. When you install Netscape Communicator, the Internet, Lookup, New&Cool, and Netcaster buttons are on the Personal toolbar by default. You can delete these buttons and add your own by displaying the desired Web site and dragging the Location icon onto the Personal toolbar.

Netscape's status indicator — Netscape's icon pulses when Netscape is processing a request (command) that you enter. To return immediately to Netscape's home page, click on this icon.

Status bar — When a Web page is opening, the Status bar indicates progress by a percentage displayed in the center and the security level of the page being loaded by a lock in the far-left corner. When you place the cursor over a hyperlink, the Status bar displays the URL of the link.

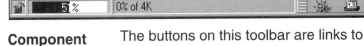

Component toolbar — The buttons on this toolbar are links to other Communicator components: Navigator, (Messenger) Mailbox, (Collabra) Discussions, and (Page) Composer.

Exit Netscape Navigator

- Exiting Netscape Navigator and disconnecting from your Internet Service Provider (ISP) are two separate steps. You can actually disconnect from your service provider and still have Netscape Navigator open. (Remember that you must first establish a connection to the Internet via your ISP to use Netscape to access information on the Web.) You can also disconnect from Navigator and still have your ISP open.

- There are times when you may want to keep Netscape open to read information obtained from the Web, access information stored on your hard disk using Netscape, or to compose e-mail to send later. If you don't disconnect from your ISP and you pay an hourly rate, you will continue incurring charges.

> **CAUTION** When you exit Netscape, you do not necessarily exit from your Internet service provider. Be sure to check the disconnect procedure from your ISP so that you will not continue to be charged for time online. Most services disconnect when a certain amount of time passes with no activity.

√ *Once you disconnect from your ISP, you can no longer access new Web information. Remember: Netscape Navigator is a browser; it is not an Internet connection.*

√ *You can disconnect from your ISP and view Web information accessed during the current session using the Back and Forward toolbar buttons. This is because the visited sites are stored in the memory of your computer. However, Web sites visited during the current session are erased from your computer memory when you exit Netscape.*

Netscape Navigator: 2

The Navigation Toolbar

■ The Netscape Navigation toolbar displays buttons for Netscape's most commonly used commands. Note that each button contains an icon and a word describing the button's function. Choosing any of these buttons activates the indicated task immediately.

■ If the Navigation toolbar is not visible, select Show Navigation Toolbar from the View menu.

 Moves back through pages previously displayed. Back is available only if you have moved around among Web pages in the current Navigator session; otherwise, it is dimmed.

 Moves forward through pages previously displayed. Forward is available only if you have used the Back button; otherwise, it is dimmed.

 Reloads the currently displayed Web page. Use this button if the current page is taking too long to display or to update the current page with any changes that may have been made since the page was downloaded.

 Displays the home page.

 Displays Netscape's Net Search Page. You can select one of several search tools from this page.

 Displays a menu with helpful links to Internet sites that contain search tools and services.

 Prints the displayed page, topic, or article.

 Displays security information for the displayed Web page as well as information on Netscape security features.

6

Stops the loading of a Web page.

URLs (Uniform Resource Locator)

■ Every Web site has a unique address called its URL (Uniform Resource Locator). A URL has four parts:

Part	Example	Description
Protocol	**http://**	The protocol indicates the method used for communicating on the internet The most common is http:// , which stands for Hypertext Transfer Protocol. Another protocol—ftp:// (file transfer protocol)—is used with internet sites designed to make files available for uploading and downloading.
Address type	**www.**	www. stands for World Wide Web and indicates that the site is located on the Web. Occasionally, you may find other address types, but www. addresses are the most common.
Identifier of the site's owner	**ddcpub**	This part of the address identifies who is responsible for the Web site.
Domain	**.com, .gov, .org, .edu, etc.** (see below)	The domain indicates the kind of organization that sponsors the site (company, government, non-profit organization, educational institution, and so on).

■ For example, the DDC publishing URL breaks down as follows:

http://www.ddcpub.com

Hypertext Transfer Protocol   World Wide Web   Company name   Domain

■ There are seven common domains:

com	Commercial enterprise	**edu**	Educational institution
org	Non-commercial organization	**mil**	U. S. Military location
net	A network that has a gateway to the Internet	**gov**	Local, state, or federal government location
int	International organization		

Open World Wide Web Sites

- There are several ways to access a Web site. If you know the site's address, you can enter the correct Web address (URL) on the Location field on the Location toolbar.

- If the address you are entering is the address of a site you have visited recently or that you have bookmarked (see "Netscape Navigator: 3" on page 9 for more information on Bookmarks), you will notice as you begin to type the address that Netscape attempts to complete it for you. If the address that Netscape suggests is the one you want, press Enter.

- If the address that Netscape suggests is not correct, keep typing to complete the desired address and then press Enter. Or, you can click the down arrow next to the Location field to view a list of other possible matches, select an address, and press Enter.

- You can also enter the URL in the Open Page dialog box. To do so, select Open Page from the File menu, select Navigator, type the URL, and click Open.

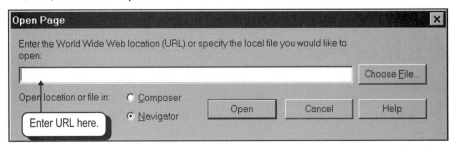

- There are a couple of shortcuts for entering URL addresses. One shortcut involves omitting the http://www. prefix from the Web address. Netscape assumes the **http://** protocol and the **www** that indicates that the site is located on the Web. If you are trying to connect to a company Web site, entering the company name is generally sufficient. Netscape assumes the **.com** suffix. For example, entering **ddcpub** on the location line and pressing Enter would reach the **http://www.ddcpub.com** address.

> √ *Don't be discouraged if the connection to the World Wide Web site is not made immediately. The site may be off-line temporarily. The site may also be very busy with others users trying to access it. Be sure the URL is typed accurately. Occasionally, it takes several tries to connect to a site.*

Netscape Navigator: 3

◆ History List ◆ Bookmarks ◆ Add Bookmarks
◆ Delete Bookmarks ◆ Print Web Pages

History List

- While you move back and forth among Web sites, Netscape automatically records each of these site locations in a **history** list, which is temporarily stored on your computer. You can use the history list to track what sites you have already visited or to jump to a recently viewed site.

  √ *As you move from one site to another on the Web, you may find yourself asking, "How did I get here?" The History list is an easy way to see the path you followed to get to the current destination.*

- To view the history list, click <u>H</u>istory on the <u>C</u>ommunicator menu, or press Ctrl+H. To link to a site shown in the history list, double-click on it.

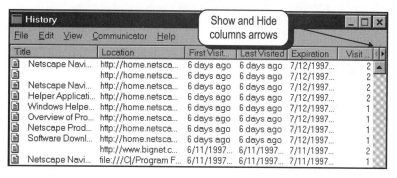

Bookmarks

- A **bookmark** is a placeholder containing the title and URL of a Web page that, when selected, links directly to that page. If you find a Web site that you like and want to revisit, you can create a bookmark to record its location. (See "Add Bookmarks" on page 10.) The Netscape bookmark feature maintains permanent records of the Web sites in your bookmark files so that you can return to them easily.

- You can view the Bookmarks menu by selecting <u>B</u>ookmarks from the <u>C</u>ommunicator menu or by clicking on the Bookmarks QuickFile button 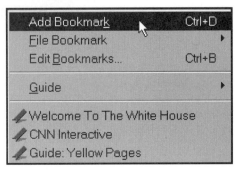 on the Location toolbar. The drop-down menu shown below appears.

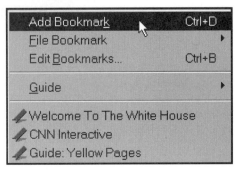

Add Bookmarks

- Display the Web page to add, go to <u>B</u>ookmarks on the <u>C</u>ommunicator menu and click Add Bookmar<u>k</u>.

Netscape does not confirm that a bookmark has been added to the file.

- You can create bookmarks from addresses in the History folder. Click <u>C</u>ommunicator, <u>H</u>istory and select the listing to bookmark. Right-click on it and choose Add To Bookmar<u>k</u>s from the menu.

Delete Bookmarks

- Bookmarks may be deleted at anytime. For example, you may wish to delete a bookmark if a Web site no longer exists or remove one that is no longer of interest to you.
- To delete a bookmark do the following:
  - Click <u>C</u>ommunicator.
  - Click <u>B</u>ookmarks.
  - Click Edit <u>B</u>ookmarks.
  - In the Bookmarks window, select the bookmark you want to delete by clicking on it from the bookmark list.
  - Press the Delete key.

OR

• Right-click on the bookmark and select <u>D</u>elete Bookmark from the drop-down menu.

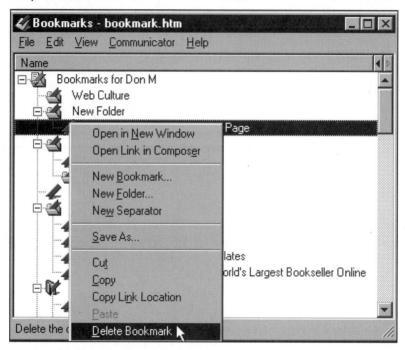

Print Web Pages

■ One of the many uses of the Internet is to print out information. You can print a page as it appears on screen, or you can print it as plain text. Only displayed pages can be printed.

■ To print a Web page, display it and do the following:

• Click the Print button on the Navigation toolbar.

OR

• Click <u>P</u>rint on the <u>F</u>ile menu.

• In the Print dialog box that displays, select the desired print options and click Print.

■ In most cases, the Web page will be printed in the format shown in the Web page display.

Netscape Messenger: 4

◆ Configure Netscape Mail ◆ Start Netscape Messenger
◆ The Message List Window ◆ Get New Mail ◆ Read Messages
◆ Delete a Message ◆ Print Messages ◆ Bookmark a Message

Configure Netscape Mail

√ *This section assumes that you have already set up an e-mail account with a service provider. If you do not have an e-mail address, contact your Internet Service Provider. Establishing a modem connection and configuring your computer to send and receive mail can be frustrating. Don't be discouraged; what follows are steps that will get you connected, but some of the information may have to be supplied by your Internet Service Provider. Calling for help will save you time and frustration.*

■ The Netscape Communicator browser suite includes a compre-hensive e-mail program called Netscape Messenger, which allows you to send, receive, save, and print e-mail messages and attachments.

■ Before you can use Messenger to send and receive e-mail, you must configure the program with your e-mail account information (user name, e-mail address, and mail server names). You may have already filled in this information if you completed the New Profile Setup Wizard when you installed Netscape Communicator.

■ You may have configured Netscape Messenger to receive and send e-mail messages when you first installed the program. If not, follow these steps to get connected. You can also use these steps to update and change settings to your e-mail account.

Identity Settings

• Open the Edit menu on the Netscape Navigator or Netscape Messenger menu and select Preferences. Click Identity in the Mail & Groups Category list to and do the following:

Enter your name and e-mail address in the first two boxes. Enter any other optional information in the Identity dialog box.

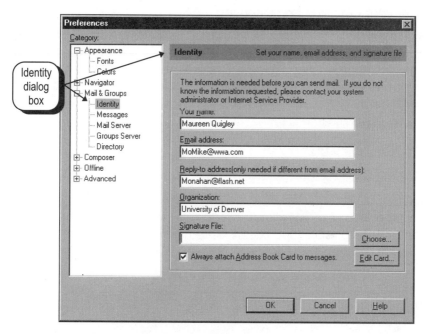

Mail Server Preference Settings

- Click Mail Server to configure your mailbox so that you can send and receive mail.

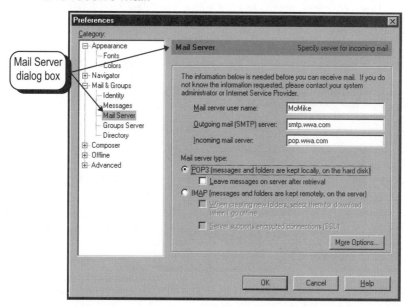

- Enter mail server user name in the first box. This is usually the part of your e-mail address that appears in front of the @ sign.

- Enter your outgoing and incoming mail server. Check with your Internet Service Provider if you are not sure what these settings are.

- Click OK to save and close the Preference settings. You should now be able to send and receive e-mail messages and/or files.

Start Netscape Messenger

■ To start Netscape Messenger:

- Click the Mailbox icon  on the Component bar.

  OR

- Start the Netscape Messenger program from the Netscape Communicator submenu on the Start menu.

📇 KMMC - More Than Words ▶	📧 Netscape Collabra
📇 Microsoft Reference ▶	🖊 Netscape Composer
📇 Movies Screen Saver ▶	📧 Netscape Conference
📇 Netscape 2.0 ▶	✴ Netscape Messenger
📇 Netscape Communicator ▶	🎞 Netscape Navigator

The Message List Window

■ After you launch Messenger, a message list window will open, displaying the contents of the e-mail Inbox folder. You can retrieve, read, forward, and reply to messages from this window.

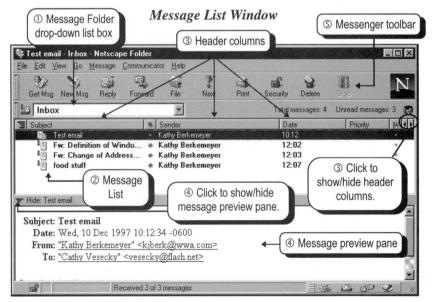

Message List Window

① Message Folder drop-down list box
③ Header columns
⑤ Messenger toolbar
② Message List
④ Click to show/hide message preview pane.
③ Click to show/hide header columns.
④ Message preview pane

14

- The message list window includes the following:

  ① The **Message Folder drop-down list box** displays the currently selected message folder, the contents of which are displayed in the message list below the drop-down box. Click the down arrow to display a list of other message folders. Select a different folder from the list to display its contents in the message list area.

  ② The **message list** displays a header for each of the messages contained in the currently selected message folder (Inbox is the default).

  ③ **Header columns** list the categories of information available for each message, such as subject, sender, and date. You can customize the display of the header columns in a number of ways:

    - Resize column widths by placing the mouse pointer over the right border of a column until the pointer changes to a double arrow, and then click and drag the border to the desired size.

    - Rearrange the order of the columns by clicking and dragging a header to a new location in the series.

    - Show/hide different columns by clicking the arrow buttons on the upper-right side of the message list window.

      √ *If text in a message header is cut off so that you cannot read it all, position the mouse pointer on the header in the column containing the cropped text. A small box will display the complete text for that column of the header, as in the example below:*

  ④ The **message preview pane** displays the content of the message currently selected from the message list. You can show/hide the preview pane by clicking on the blue triangle icon in the bottom-left corner of the message list pane. You can resize the preview pane or the message list pane by placing the pointer over the border between the two panes until the pointer changes to a double arrow and then dragging the border up or down to the desired size.

  ⑤ The **Messenger toolbar** displays buttons for activating Netscape Messenger's most commonly used commands. Note that each button contains an image and a word describing the function. Choosing any of these buttons will activate the indicated task immediately.

Messenger Toolbar Buttons and Functions

 Retrieves new mail from your Internet mail server and loads it into the Inbox message folder.

 Opens the Message Composition screen allowing you to compose new mail messages.

 Allows you to reply to the sender of an e-mail message or to the sender and all other recipients of the e-mail message.

 Forwards a message you have received to another address.

 Stores the current message in one of six Messenger default file folders or in a new folder that you create.

 Selects and displays the next of the unread messages in your Inbox.

 Prints the displayed message.

 Displays the security status of a message.

 Deletes the selected message. Deleted messages are moved to the Trash folder. You must delete contents of Trash folder to remove messages from your computer.

Get New Mail

- Since new e-mail messages are stored on a remote ISP mail server, you must be connected to the Internet to access them. To retrieve new messages to your computer, click the Get Msg button on the Messenger toolbar.

- In the Password Entry dialog box that follows, enter your e-mail password in the blank text box and click OK. (If you do not know your e-mail password, contact your ISP.)

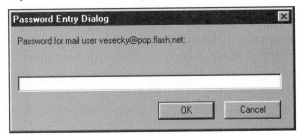

√ *Messenger saves your password for the rest of the current Messenger session. You must re-enter it each time you retrieve new mail, unless you set Messenger to save your password permanently. To do so:*

- Click Edit, Preferences.
- Click once on Mail Server under Mail & Groups.
- Click the More Options button.
- Select the Remember my mail password check box and click OK twice.

■ The Getting New Messages box opens, displaying the status of your message retrieval.

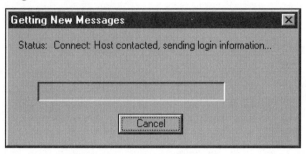

■ Once your new messages are retrieved, they are listed in the message list window. By default, Messenger stores new mail messages in the Inbox folder.

Read Messages

■ You can read a message in the preview pane of the message list window or in a separate window.

■ To read a message in the preview pane, click on the desired message header in the message list. If the message does not appear, click on the blue triangle icon at the bottom of the message list window to display the preview pane.

■ To open and read a message in a separate window, double-click on the desired message header in the message list. You can close a message after reading it by clicking File, Close or by clicking on the Close button (X) in the upper-right corner of the window.

■ To read the next unread message, click the Next button on the Messenger toolbar. Or, if you have reached the end of the current message, you can press the spacebar to proceed to the next unread message.

■ Once you have read a message, it remains stored in the Inbox folder until you delete it or file it in another folder. (See "Delete a Message" below.)

√ *You do not have to be online to read e-mail. You can reduce your online charges if you disconnect from your ISP after retrieving your messages and read them offline.*

√ *Icons located to the left of message headers in the message list identify each message as either unread* ✉ *(retrieved during a previous Messenger session), new* 📥 *(and unread), or read* 📭.

Delete a Message

■ To delete a message, select its header from the message list window and click the Delete button ⬚ Delete ⬚ in the Messenger toolbar.

√ *To select more than one message to delete, click the Ctrl button while you click each message header.*

Print Messages

■ In order to print a message you must first display the message in either the preview pane of the message list window or in a separate window, then:

• Click the Print button ⬚ Print ⬚ on the Messenger toolbar.

• In the Print dialog box that appears, select the desired print options and click OK.

Print Dialog Box

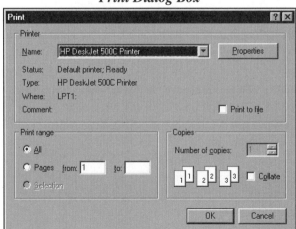

18

Bookmark a Message

■ You can add an e-mail message to your Bookmarks folder for easy access from anywhere within the Communicator suite. To bookmark a message:

- Display the message you want to bookmark in either the preview pane of the message list window or in a separate window.

- Select Communicator, Bookmarks, Add Bookmark.

■ Messenger will add the message to the bottom of your Bookmarks menu.

Netscape Messenger: 5

◆ **Compose New Messages** ◆ **Send Messages**
◆ **The Message Composition Toolbar** ◆ **Reply to Mail**
◆ **Forward Mail** ◆ **Add Entries to the Personal Address Book**
◆ **Address a New Message Using the Personal Address Book**

Compose New Messages

■ You can compose an e-mail message in Netscape Messenger while
you are connected to the Internet, or while you are offline. When
composing an e-mail message online, you can send the message
immediately after creating it. When composing a message offline
(which is considered proper Netiquette—net etiquette), you will
need to store the message in your Unsent Messages folder until
you are online and can send it.

■ To create a message, you first need to open Messenger's Message
Composition window. To do so:

● Click the New Message button [New Msg].

√ *The Message Composition window displays.*

Netscape Message Composition Window

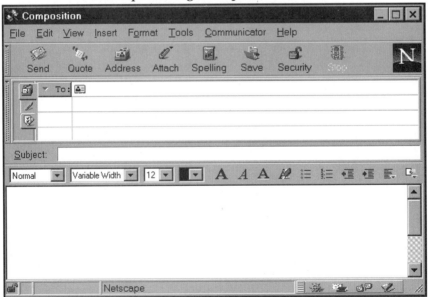

√ *You can hide any toolbar in the Message Composition screen by going to View, Hide Message Toolbar or Hide Formatting Toolbar.*

√ *If you do not know the recipient's address, you can look it up and insert it from your personal address book (see page 24) or an online directory.*

■ In the Message Composition window, type the Internet address(es) of the message recipient(s) in the To: field. Or, click the Address

button [Address] on the Message Composition toolbar and select an address to insert (see pages 24-26 for more information on using the Address Book).

√ *If you are sending the message to multiple recipients, press Enter after typing each recipient's address.*

■ After inserting the address(es), click the To: icon [To:] to display a drop-down menu of other addressee options. Select any of the following options from the drop-down menu and enter the recipient information indicated.

To	The e-mail address of the person to whom the message is being sent.
CC (Carbon Copy)	The e-mail addresses of people who will receive copies of the message.
BCC (Blind Carbon Copy)	Same as CC, except these names will not appear anywhere in the message, so other recipients will not know that the person(s) listed in the BCC field received a copy.
Group	Names of newsgroups that will receive this message (similar to Mail To).
Reply To	The e-mail address where replies should be sent.
Follow-up To	Another newsgroup heading; used to identify newsgroups to which comments should be posted (similar to Reply To).

■ Click in the Subject field (or press Tab to move the cursor there) and type the subject of the message.

■ Click in the blank composition area below the Subject field and type the body of your message. Word wrap occurs automatically, and you can cut and paste quotes from other messages or text from other programs. You can also check the spelling of your message by clicking on the Spelling button  on the Message Composition toolbar and responding to the dialog prompts that follow.

Send Messages

■ Once you have created a message, you have three choices:

- to send the message immediately
- to store the message in the Unsent Messages folder to be sent later (File, Send Later)
- to save the message in the Drafts folder to be finished and sent later (File, Save Draft)

To send a message immediately:

- Click the Send button Send on the Message Composition toolbar.

The Message Composition Toolbar

■ The toolbar in the Message Composition window has several features that are specific only to this screen.

■ Notice that the main toolbar buttons contain a task name and illustration.

Message Composition Toolbar

	Immediately sends current message.
	Used when replying to a message, the Quote feature allows you to include text from the original message.
	Select an address from the addresses stored in your personal address book to insert into address fields.
	By clicking the Attach button, you can send a file, a Web page, or your personal address card along with your e-mail message.
	Checks for spelling errors in the current message.

Lets you save your message as a draft for later use.

 Sets the security status of a message.

 Stops the display of an HTML message or a message with an HTML attachment.

- The Formatting toolbar provides commands for applying styles, fonts, font size, bulleted lists, and inserting objects.

Reply to Mail

- To reply to a message, select or open the message to reply to and

  click the Reply button [Reply].

- From the submenu that appears, select Reply to Sender to reply to the original sender only, or select Reply to Sender and All Recipients to send a reply to the sender and all other recipients of the original message. Selecting one of these options lets you reply to the message without having to enter the recipient's name or e-mail address.

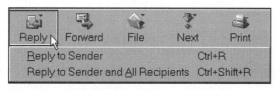

√ *The Message Composition window opens, with the To, Cc, and Subject fields filled in for you.*

- Compose your reply as you would a new message.

- To include a copy of the original message with your reply, click the

  Quote button [Quote] on the Message Composition toolbar. You can edit the original message and header text as you wish.

- When you are finished, click the Send button [Send] to send the message immediately.

Forward Mail

■ To forward a message automatically without having to enter the recipient's name or e-mail address, first select or open the message to forward. Then click on the Forward button ⬚ Forward .

The Message Composition window opens, with the Subject field filled in for you.

Subject: [Fwd: Andy's Birthday Party]

■ Type the e-mail address of the new recipient in the To field, or click the Address button ⬚ Address on the Message Composition toolbar and select a name from your Address Book (see "Address a New Message Using the Personal Address Book" on page 26 for information on using the Address Book).

■ If the original message does not appear in the composition area, click the Quote button ⬚ Quote on the Message Composition toolbar to insert it.

■ Click in the composition area and edit the message as desired. You can also type any additional text you want to include with the forwarded message.

■ When you are done, click the Send button ⬚ Send to send the message immediately. Or, select Send Later from the File menu to store the message in the Unsent Messages mailbox to be sent later. To save the reply as a draft to be edited and sent later, select Save Draft from the File menu.

Add Entries to the Personal Address Book

■ You can compile a personal address book to store e-mail addresses and other information about your most common e-mail recipients. You can then use the address book to find and automatically insert an address when creating a new message.

■ To add a name to the address book:

• Select Address Book from the Communicator menu. The Address Book window displays.

24

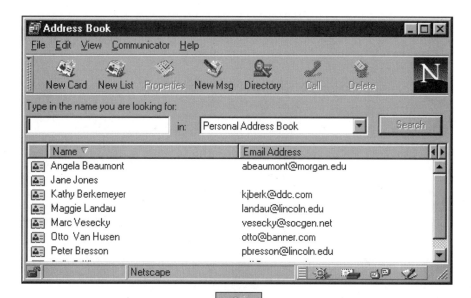

- Click the New Card button 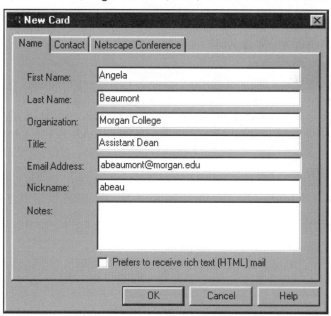 on the Address Book toolbar.
- In the New Card box that appears, enter the recipient's first name, last name, organization, title, and e-mail address.

- In the Nickname field, type a nickname for the recipient, if desired (the nickname must be unique among the entries in your address book). When addressing a message, you can use the recipient's nickname in the To field, rather than typing the entire address, and Messenger will automatically fill in the full e-mail address.

- In the Notes field, type any notes you want to store about the recipient.

- Click the Contact tab, if desired, and enter the recipient's postal address and phone number.

- Click OK.

■ You can edit an address book entry at any time by double-clicking on the person's name in the Address Book window.

■ You can automatically add the name and address of the sender of a message you are reading by selecting Add to Address Book from the Message menu and selecting Sender from the submenu. The New Card dialog box opens, with the First Name, Last Name, and E-mail Address fields filled in for you. You can enter a nickname for the person, if desired, and any other information you want in the remaining fields.

Address a New Message Using the Personal Address Book

■ To insert an address from your address book into a new message:

- Click the New Msg button to open the Message Composition window.

- Click on the Address button on the Message Composition toolbar and select a recipient(s) from the list in the Address Book window. Drag the selected name(s) into the To field in the Message Composition window. Click the Close button in the Address Book window when you are finished.

OR

- Begin typing the name or nickname of the recipient in the To field of the Message Composition window. If the name is included in the Address Book, Messenger will recognize it and finish entering the name and address for you.

◆ **Attached Files** ◆ **View File Attachments**
◆ **Save Attached Files** ◆ **Attach Files to Messages**

Attached Files

■ Sometimes an e-mail message will come with a separate file(s) attached. Messages containing attachments are indicated when you

display a message and it contains a paperclip icon to the right of the message header. Attachment can be used, for example, when you want to send someone an Excel spreadsheet or a video clip.

■ With Messenger, you can view both plain text attachments and binary attachments. **Binary** files are files containing more than plain text (i.e., images, sound clips, and formatted text, such as spreadsheets and word processor documents).

■ Almost any e-mail program can read plain text files. Binary files, however, must be decoded by the receiving e-mail program before they can be displayed in readable form. This requires that the e-mail software have the capability to decode either MIME (Multi-Purpose Internet Mail Extension) or UUEncode protocol. Messenger can decode both. When a binary attachment arrives, Messenger automatically recognizes and decodes it.

View File Attachments

■ File or HTML attachments are displayed in one of two ways.

• If you select View, Attachments, Inline, you see the attachment appended to the body of the message in a separate attachment window below the message. Essentially there is a series of sequential windows—one with the message and the other with the attachment.

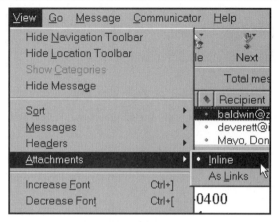

√ *Only plain text, images, and Web page attachments can be viewed inline.*

• If the attachment is HTML code, you will see a fully formatted Web page.

• If you select View, Attachments, As Links, the attachment window displays an attachment box displaying the details of the attachment. It also serves as a link to the attachment.

√ *Viewing attachments as links reduces the time it takes to open a message on screen.*

• Clicking on the blue-highlighted text in the attachment box will display the attachment.

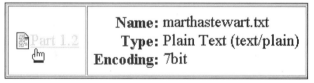

Name: marthastewart.txt
Type: Plain Text (text/plain)
Encoding: 7bit

■ You can right-click on the attachment icon box to display a menu of mail options such as forwarding, replying, or deleting the message.

• By right-clicking on the actual attachment, you can choose from several file save options, such as saving the image or file in a separate file on your hard drive, as Windows wallpaper, or saving the image and putting a shortcut to the image on your desktop.

• If you open a Web page attachment while online, you will find that the Web page serves as an actual connection to the Web site and that all links on the page are active. If you are not connected, the Web page will display fully formatted, but it will not be active.

■ If an attached image displays as a link even after you select View, Attachments, Inline, it is probably because it is an image type that Messenger does not recognize. In this case, you need to install and/or open a plug-in or program with which to view the unrecognized image.

■ If you know you have the appropriate application or plug-in installed, click the Save File button in the Unknown File Type dialog box and save the attachment to your hard drive or disk (see "Save Attached Files" below). Then start the necessary application or plug-in and open the saved attachment file to view it.

■ If you do not have the necessary application or plug-in, click on the More Info button in the Unknown File Type dialog box. The Netscape Plug-in Finder Web page opens, displaying some general information about plug-ins, a list of plug-ins that will open the selected attachment, and hyperlinks to Web sites where you can download the given plug-ins.

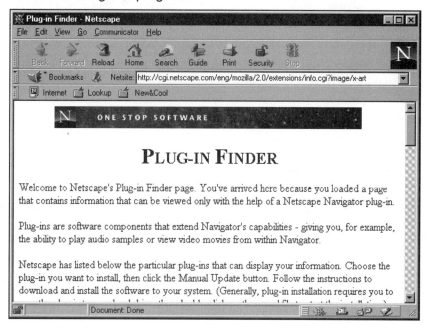

Save Attached Files

■ You can save an attached file to your hard drive or disk for future use or reference. To save an attachment:

• Open the message containing the attachment to save.

• If the attachment is in inline view, convert it to a link (View, Attachments, As Links).

• Right-click on the link and select Save Link As.

OR

- Click on the link to open the attachment. Select File, Save As, or, if Messenger does not recognize the attachment's file type, click the Save File button in the Unknown File Type dialog box.

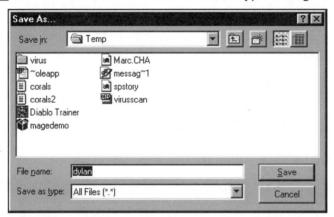

- In the Save As dialog box that follows, click the Save in drop-down list box and select the drive and folder(s) in which to save the file.
- Click in the File name text box and type a name for the file.
- Click Save.

Attach Files to Messages

- With Messenger, you can attach both plain text and binary files (images, media clips, formatted text documents, etc.) to e-mail messages. You may wish to check if your recipient's e-mail software can decode MIME or UUEncode protocols. Otherwise, binary attachments will not open and display properly on the recipient's computer.

- To attach a file to an e-mail message:

  - Click the Attach button [Attach] on the Message Composition toolbar, and select File from the drop-down menu that appears.

  - In the Enter file to attach dialog box that follows, click the Look in drop-down list box and select the drive and folder containing the file to attach.

  - Then select the file to attach and click Open.

- After you have attached a file, the Attachments field in the Mail Composition window displays the name and location of the attached file.

  √ *Messages containing attachments usually take longer to send than those without attachments. When attaching very large files or multiple files, you may want to zip (compress) the files before attaching them. To do so, both you and the recipient need a file compression program, such as WinZip or PKZip.*

Attach Files and Documents

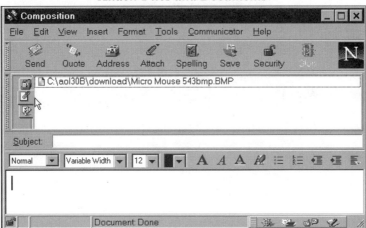

- Once you have attached the desired files and finished composing your message, you can send the e-mail, save it in the Unsent Messages folder for later delivery, or save it as a draft for later editing.

Microsoft Internet Explorer: 7

◆ **Start Internet Explorer 4**
◆ **Internet Explorer Screen** ◆ **Exit Internet Explorer**

Start Internet Explorer 4

■ When you first install Internet Explorer and you are using the Active Desktop, you may see the message illustrated below when you turn on your computer. If you are familiar with Explorer 3, you may want to select 1 Take a Quick Tour to learn the new features in Explorer 4. Select 2 to learn about Channels.

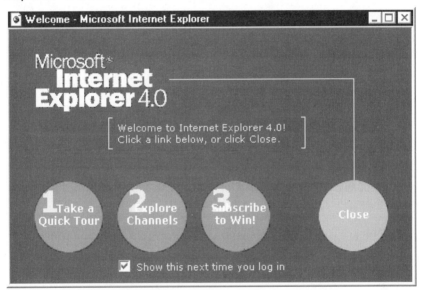

■ To start Internet Explorer, do one of the following:

  • Click [Internet Explorer icon] on the Desktop.

    OR

  • Click [icon] on the taskbar.

    OR

  • Click the Start button [Start], then select Programs, Internet Explorer, and click Internet Explorer.

Internet Explorer Screen

- When you connect to the World Wide Web, the first screen that displays is called a home page. The term home page can be misleading since the first page of *any* World Wide Web site is called a home page. This first page is also sometimes referred to as the start page. You could think of the home/start page as the starting point of your trip on the information highway. Just as you can get on a highway using any number of on ramps, you can get on the Internet at different starting points.

- You can change the first page that you see when you connect to the Internet. To do this select View, Internet Options, then enter a new address in the Address text box.

   √ *The page that you see when you are connected may differ from the one illustrated below.*

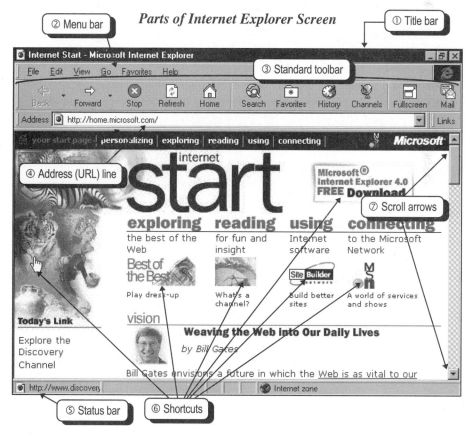

Parts of Internet Explorer Screen

① **Title bar**   Displays the name of the program and the current Web page. You can minimize, restore, or close Explorer using the buttons on the right side of the Title bar.

② **Menu bar**   Displays menus currently available, which provide drop-down lists of commands for executing Internet Explorer tasks.

     The Internet Explorer icon on the right side of the Menu bar rotates when action is occurring or information is being processed.

③ **Standard toolbar**   Displays frequently used commands.

④ **Address (URL) line**   Displays the address of the current page. You can click here, type a new address, press Enter, and go to a new location (if it's an active Web site). You can also start a search from this line.

If you click on the arrow at the right end of the address line, you will see the links that you have visited during the current Internet session. The Links bar, containing links to various Microsoft sites is concealed on the right side of the address bar. Drag the split bar to the left or somewhere else on the screen to display current Links. If you double-click the Links button, all the current links will display. Double-click again to hide the links on the right side of the menu bar. You can add/delete links.

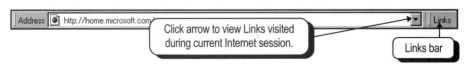

Note in the illustration above that the Links button has moved to the left side of the address bar. Just double-click on the Links button again to restore the address line. You can also drag the move bar, next to the Links button, to the left so that the Links and the Address line will both display. Drag the Links button down to display the contents of the Links bar directly below the Address bar (see illustration below).

⑤ **Status bar**   Displays information about actions occurring on the page and the Security Level. Internet Security Properties lets you control content that is downloaded on to your computer.

⑥ **Shortcuts**   Click on shortcuts (also called hyperlinks) to move to other Web sites. Shortcuts are usually easy to recognize. They can be underlined text, text of different colors, "buttons" of various sizes and shapes, or graphics. An easy way to tell if you are pointing to a shortcut is by watching the mouse pointer as it moves over the page. When it changes to a hand, you are on a shortcut. When you point to a shortcut the full name of the Web site will appear on the Status bar.

⑦ **Scroll arrows**   Scroll arrows are used to move the screen view, as in all Windows applications.

Exit Internet Explorer

■ Exiting Internet Explorer and disconnecting from your service
provider are two separate steps. It is important to remember that if
you close Internet Explorer (or any other browser), you must also
disconnect (or hang up) from your service provider. If you don't
disconnect, you'll continue incurring charges.

> **CAUTION** *When you exit Internet Explorer, you do not
> necessarily exit from your Internet service provider. Be
> sure to check the disconnect procedure from your ISP
> so that you will not continue to be charged for time
> online. Some services automatically disconnect when
> a specific amount of time has passed with no activity.*

Microsoft Internet Explorer: 8

◆ **Standard Toolbar Buttons**
◆ **Open a World Wide Web Site from the Address Bar**
◆ **Open a World Wide Web Site Using the File Open Dialog Box**

Internet Explorer Toolbar

Standard Toolbar Buttons

■ The **Internet Explorer Standard toolbar** displays frequently used commands. If the Standard toolbar is *not* visible when you start Explorer, open the View menu, select Toolbars, then select Standard Buttons.

 Moves back through pages previously displayed. Back is available only if you have moved around among Web pages in the current Navigator session; otherwise, it is dimmed.

 Moves forward through pages previously displayed. Forward is available only if you have used the Back button; otherwise, it is dimmed.

 Interrupts the opening of a page that is taking too long to display. Some pages are so filled with graphics, audio, or video clips that delays can be expected.

 Reloads the current page.

 Returns you to your home page. You can change your home page to open to any Web site or a blank page (View, Internet Options, General).

 Allows you to select from a number of search services with a variety of options.

 Displays the Web sites that you have stored using the features available on the Favorites menu. Click Favorites button again to close the Favorites.

Displays links to Web sites that you have visited in previous days and weeks. You can change the number of days that sites are stored in your History folder (View, Internet Options). Click the History button again to close the History window.

Displays the list of current channels on the Explorer bar. Click again to close the Channels window.

Conceals Menu, titles, Status bar, and address line to make available the maximum screen space possible for viewing a Web page. Click it again to restore Menu, titles, Status bar, and address line.

Displays a drop-down menu with various Mail and News options. You will learn about Outlook Express e-mail options in Chapters 10-12.

Open a World Wide Web Site from the Address Bar

■ Click in the Address bar and start typing the address of the Web site you want to open. If you have visited the site before, Internet Explorer will try to complete the address automatically. If it is the correct address, press Enter to go to it. If it is not the correct address, type over the suggested address that displayed on the line. To see other possible matches, click the down arrow. If you find the one you want, click on it.

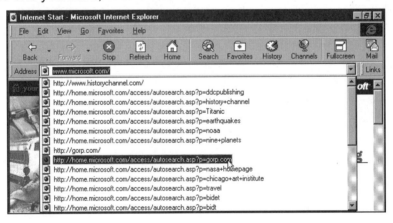

■ To turn off the AutoComplete feature, open the View menu, select Internet Options, and click the Advanced tab. Deselect Use AutoComplete in the Browsing area of the dialog box.

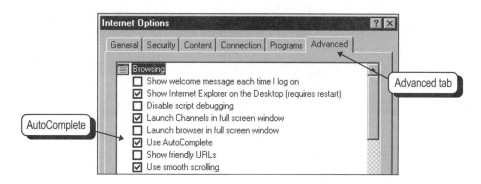

Open a World Wide Web Site Using the File Open Dialog Box

■ Select File, Open, and start entering the exact address of the site you want to open. If AutoComplete is turned on and Explorer finds a potential match for the site, it will automatically appear on this line. If the match is the site you want to open, press Enter to go there. If you want to see other possible matches, click the down arrow in the open dialog box.

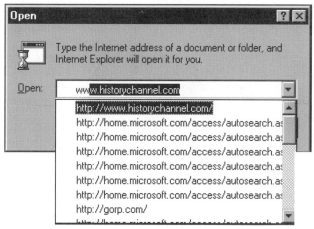

√ *Other ways of opening Web sites will be explored in this lesson. Chapters 19-21 will explain how to search for sites whose exact addresses you do not know.*

◆ **Open and Add to the Favorites Folder**
◆ **Open Web Sites from the Favorites Folder**
◆ **Create New Folders in the Favorites Folder**
◆ **AutoSearch from the Address Bar**

Open and Add to the Favorites Folder

■ As you spend more time exploring Web sites, you will find sites that you want to visit frequently. You can store shortcuts to these sites in the **Favorites folder**.

■ To add a site to the Favorites folder, first go to the desired Web site. Open the F̲avorites menu or right-click anywhere on the page and select Add To F̲avorites.

■ The following dialog box appears when you select Add to F̲avorites.

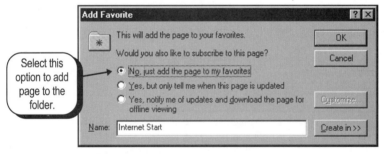

Select this option to add page to the folder.

■ The name of the Page you have opened appears in the N̲ame box. There are three ways you can store the address in response to the question "Would you also like to subscribe to this page?" Subscribing to a page means you can schedule automatic updates to that site.

- N̲o, just add the page to my favorites
  Puts a shortcut to the Web site in your Favorites folder.

- Y̲es, but only tell me when this page is updated
  Explorer will alert you when an update to the site is available.

- Yes, notify me of updates and d̲ownload the page for offline viewing
  Explorer will automatically download and update to your computer.

■ Click OK to add the Web address to the Favorites folder.

Open Web Sites from the Favorites Folder

- Click the Favorites button [Favorites] on the Standard toolbar to open Web sites from the Favorites folder. The Explorer bar will open on the left side of the Browser window.

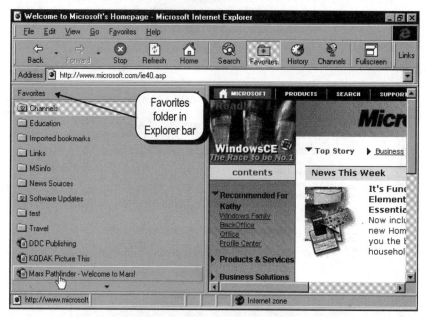

- Click on an address or open a folder and select a site. Close the Explorer bar by clicking the close button or the Favorites button on the toolbar.

- You can also open the Favorites menu and select a site from the list or from a folder.

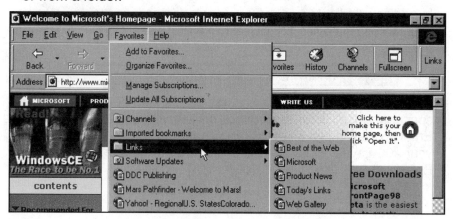

Create New Folders in the Favorites Folder

- You can create new folders before or after you have saved addresses in your Favorites folder.
  - Click Favorites and select Organize Favorites.
  - Click the Create New Folder button (shown in illustration below).

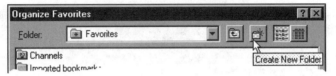

  - Type the name of the new folder and press Enter.

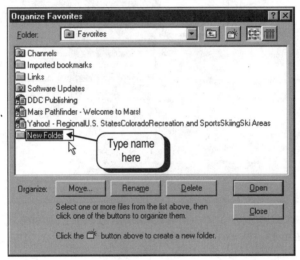

AutoSearch from the Address Bar

- In addition to displaying and entering addresses in the Address bar, you can use AutoSearch to perform a quick search directly from the Address bar.

- Click once in the Address bar and type *go, find,* or *?* and press the spacebar once. Enter the word or phrase you want to find and press Enter. For example, if you want to search for information about the year 2000, type "Find the year 2000" on the Address bar and press Enter.

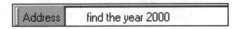

- Note the Status bar displays the message "Finding site…" It is actually finding a search site. In a few moments, the results of your search displays. The keywords in your search appear in bold in the list of links that are relevant to the search string that you entered.

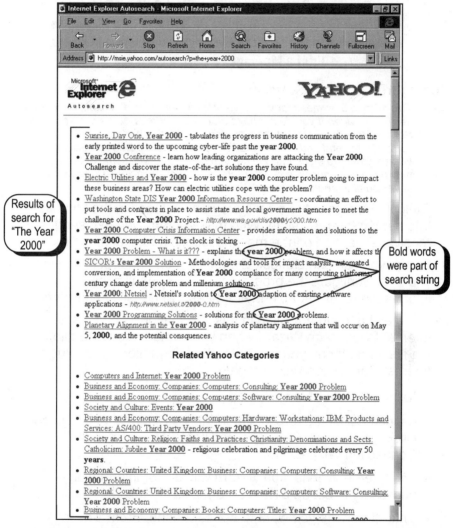

- AutoSearch uses only one search site. If you want to refine your search or see if other search engines will give you different results,

click the Search button [Search] on the Standard toolbar and select a Search provider from the Choose provider drop-down list in the Explorer bar to access a different Search site.

Outlook Express: 10

Configure Outlook Express

√ *This section assumes that you have already set up an e-mail account with a service provider. If you do not have an e-mail address, contact your Internet Service Provider. Establishing a modem connection and configuring your computer to send and receive mail can be frustrating. Don't be discouraged. What follows are steps that will get you connected, but some of the information may have to be supplied by your Internet Service Provider. Calling for help will save you time and frustration.*

■ Outlook Express is the e-mail program included in the Microsoft Internet Explorer 4.0 suite. With this program, you can send, receive, save, and print e-mail messages and attachments.

■ Before you can use Outlook Express to send and receive e-mail, you must configure the program with your e-mail account information (user name, e-mail address, and mail server names).

■ You may have already filled in this information if you completed the Internet Connection Wizard when you started Internet Explorer for the first time. If not, you can enter the information by running the Internet Connection Wizard again.

Internet Connection Wizard

• Launch Outlook Express. Open the Tools menu, select Accounts. Click the Mail tab. Click Add and select Mail to start the Connection Wizard.

• The Internet Connection Wizard will ask for information necessary to set up or add an e-mail account.

• Enter the name you want to appear on the "From" line in your outgoing messages. Click Next.

44

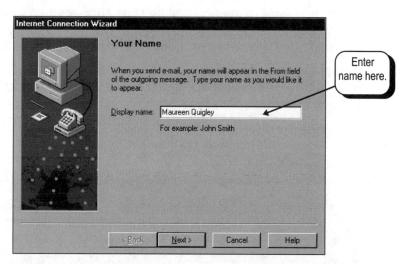

- Type your e-mail address. This is the address that people use to send mail to you. You usually get to create the first part of the address (the portion in front of the @ sign); the rest is assigned by your Internet Service Provider. Click Next.

- Enter the names of your incoming and outgoing mail servers. Check with your Internet Service Provider if you do not know what they are. Click Next.

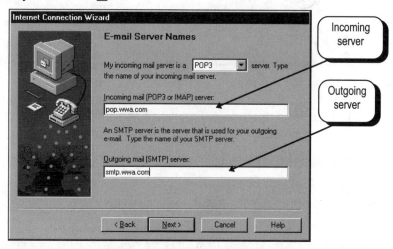

- Enter the logon name that your Internet Service Provider requires for you to access your mail. You will probably also have to enter a password. The password will appear as asterisks (******) to prevent others from knowing it. Click Next when you are finished.

- Enter the name of the account that will appear when you open the <u>A</u>ccounts list on the <u>T</u>ools menu in Outlook Express. It can be any name that you choose. Click <u>N</u>ext when you have finished.

- Select the type of connection that you are using to reach the Internet. If you are connecting through a phone line, you will need to have a dial-up connection. If you have an existing connection, click <u>N</u>ext and select from the list of current connections.

- Select an existing dial-up connection, or select <u>C</u>reate a new dial-up connection and follow the directions to create a new one.

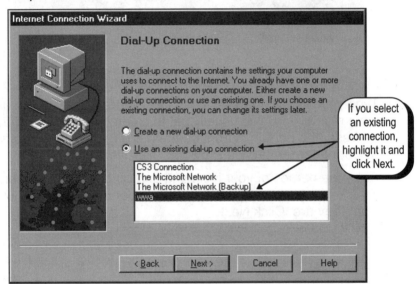

- If you select <u>U</u>se an existing dial-up connection you will click Finish in the last window to save the settings. You should then be able to launch Outlook Express and send and receive mail and attachments.

Start Outlook Express

■ To start Outlook Express:

- Click the Mail icon [icon] on the taskbar.

  √ *There is a chance that clicking the Mail icon from the Explorer main window will take you to the Microsoft Outlook organizational program. To use the more compact Outlook Express as your default mail program, click <u>V</u>iew, Internet <u>O</u>ptions from the Explorer main window. Click the Programs tab and choose Outlook Express from the <u>M</u>ail pull-down menu.*

  √ *If you downloaded Internet Explorer 4, be sure that you downloaded the standard version, which includes Outlook Express in addition to the Web browser.*

46

Outlook Express Main Window

■ After you launch Outlook Express, the main Outlook Express window opens by default. You can access any e-mail function from this window.

Outlook Express Main Window

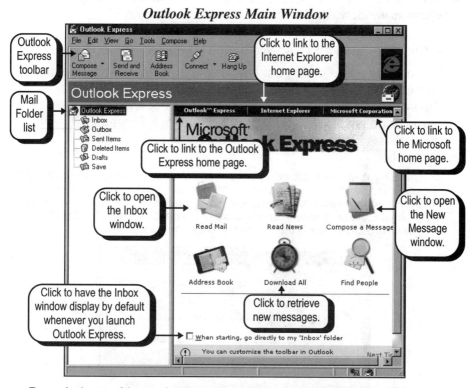

■ Descriptions of items in the main window follow below:

  • The **Mail Folder list** displays in the left column of the window, with the Outlook Express main folder selected. To view the contents of a different folder, click on the desired folder in the folder list.

  • **Shortcuts** to different e-mail functions are located in the center of the window. Click once on a shortcut to access the indicated task or feature.

  • **Hyperlinks** to Microsoft home pages are located at the top of the window. Click once to connect to the indicated home page.

  • The **Outlook Express toolbar** displays buttons for commonly used commands. Note that each button contains an image and text that describes the button function. Move your cursor over the button to display specific function information. Clicking any of these buttons will activate the indicated task immediately.

Retrieve New Messages

■ You can access the retrieve new mail command from any Outlook Express window. To do so:

• Click the Send and Receive button 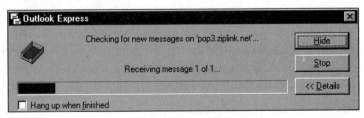 on the toolbar.

■ In the Connection dialog box that displays, enter your ISP user name in the Underline User Name text box and your password in the Password text box and click OK. (If you do not know your user name or password, contact your ISP.) Outlook Express will send this information to your ISP's mail server in order to make a connection.

√ *Outlook Express will automatically save your user name and password for the rest of the current Internet session. However, you must re-enter your password each time you reconnect to the Internet or retrieve new mail, unless you set Outlook Express to save your password permanently. To do so, select the* **Save Password** *check box in the connection dialog box and click OK.*

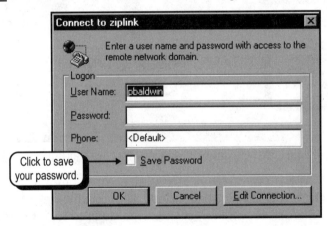

■ Once you are connected to the Internet and Outlook Express is connected to your ISP mail server, new mail messages will begin downloading from your ISP mail server. A dialog box displays the status of the transmittal.

The Mail Window

- After retrieving new messages, Outlook Express stores them in the Inbox folder.

- To view your new messages, you must open the Mail window and display the contents of the Inbox folder. To do so:

  - Click the Read Mail shortcut [Read Mail] in the Outlook Express main window.

- The Mail window opens with the Inbox folder displayed. A description of the items in the Mail window appears on the following page:

Mail Window with Inbox Folder Displayed

√ *In the message list, unread messages are displayed in bold text with a sealed envelope icon to the left of the header. Messages that have been read are listed in regular text with an open envelope icon to the left of the header.*

① The **Mail Folder list** displays the currently selected message folder, the contents of which are displayed in the mail list. Click on another folder to display its contents in the mail list.

② The **message list pane** displays a header for each of the messages contained in the currently selected mail folder.

③ **Column headings** list the categories of information included in each message header, such as subject, from, and date received. You can customize the display of the header columns in a number of ways:

- Resize column widths by placing the mouse pointer over the right border of a column heading until the pointer changes to a double arrow and then click and drag the border to the desired size.

- Rearrange the order of the columns by clicking and dragging a column heading to a new location in the series.

④ The **preview pane** displays the content of the message currently selected from the message list. You can show/hide the preview pane by selecting View, Layout and clicking on the Use preview pane check box. You can resize the preview pane or the message list pane by placing the pointer over the border between the two panes until the pointer changes to a double arrow and then dragging the border up or down to the desired size.

⑤ The **Mail toolbar** displays command buttons for working with messages. These commands vary depending on the message folder currently displayed (Inbox, Sent, Outbox, etc.).

Read Messages

√ *You do not have to be online to read e-mail. You can reduce your online charges if you disconnect from your ISP after retrieving your messages and read them offline.*

■ You must have the Mail window open and the mail folder containing the message to read displayed.

■ You can read a message in the preview pane of the Mail window, or in a separate window.

■ To read a message in the preview pane, click on the desired message header in the message list. If the message does not appear, select View, Layout, Use preview pane.

■ To open and read a message in a separate window, double-click on the desired message header in the message list.

√ *The Message window opens displaying the Message toolbar and the contents of the selected message.*

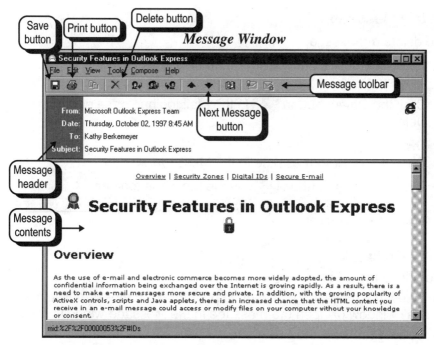

Message Window

- You can close the Message window after reading a message by clicking File, Close or by clicking on the Close button (X) in the upper-right corner of the window.

- Use the scroll bars in the Message window or the preview pane to view hidden parts of a displayed message. Or, press the down arrow key to scroll down through the message.

- To read the next unread message:

  • Select View, Next, Next Unread Message.

  OR

  • If you are viewing a message in the Message window, click the Next button ▼ on the Message toolbar.

- Once you have read a message, it remains stored in the Inbox folder until you delete it or file it in another folder. (See "Delete a Message" on the following page.)

Delete a Message

■ To delete a message:

• Select the desired header from the message list in the Mail window.

• Click the Delete button 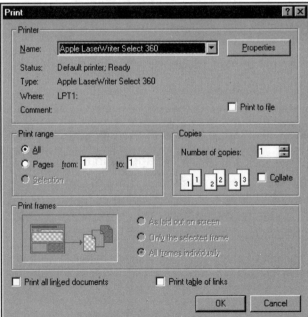 in the Mail toolbar, or select <u>E</u>dit, <u>D</u>elete.

OR

• Open the desired message in the Message window.

• Click the Delete button ☒ on the Message toolbar.

√ *To select more than one message to delete, click the Ctrl button while you click each message header.*

Print a Message

■ To print a message:

• Select the message you want to print from the message list in the Mail window or open the message in the Message window.

• Select <u>P</u>rint from the <u>F</u>ile menu.

• In the Print dialog box that opens, select the desired print options and click OK.

Print Dialog Box

Print	? ☒
Printer	
Name:	Apple LaserWriter Select 360 ▼	Properties
Status:	Default printer; Ready
Type:	Apple LaserWriter Select 360
Where:	LPT1:
Comment:	☐ Print to file

Print range
⊙ All
○ Pages from: 1 to: 1
○ Selection

Copies
Number of copies: 1
☐ Collate

Print frames
○ As laid out on screen
○ Only the selected frame
⊙ All frames individually

☐ Print all linked documents   ☐ Print table of links

OK   Cancel

■ You can bypass the Print dialog box and send the message to the printer using the most recently used print settings by opening the message in the Message window and clicking the Print button  on the Message toolbar.

Save a Message

■ To save a message to your hard drive:

• Open the desired message in the Message window and click the Save button 🖫 on the Message toolbar.

• In the Save Message As dialog box that opens, click the Save in drop-down list box and select the drive and folder in which to store the message file.

Save Messages As

• Click in the File name box and enter a name for the message.
• Click Save.

◆ **Compose New Messages** ◆ **Send Messages** ◆ **Reply to Mail**
◆ **Forward Mail** ◆ **Add Entries to the Personal Address Book**
◆ **Address a New Message Using the Personal Address Book**

Compose New Messages

■ You can compose an e-mail message in Outlook Express while you are connected to the Internet, or while you are offline. When composing an e-mail message online, you can send the message immediately after creating it. When composing a message offline, you will need to store the message in your Outbox folder until you are online and can send it. (See "Send Messages" on page 56.)

■ To create a message, you first need to open the New Message window. To do so:

- Click the New Mail Message button ![Compose Message] on the toolbar in either the Mail window or the Main window.

  The New Message window displays (see the next page).

  √ *You can hide any toolbar in the New Message window by going to the View menu and deselecting Toolbar, Formatting Toolbar, or Status Bar.*

- In the New Message window, type the Internet address(es) of the message recipient(s) in the To field.

  √ *If you type the first few characters of a name or e-mail address that is saved in your address book, Outlook Express will automatically complete it for you. (See page 60 for information on using the Address Book.)*

  OR

  Click the Index Card icon ![Index Card] in the To field or the Address Book

  button ![Address Book] on the New Message toolbar and select an address to insert (see page 60 for information on using the Address Book).

  √ *If you are sending the message to multiple recipients, insert a comma or semicolon between each recipient's address.*

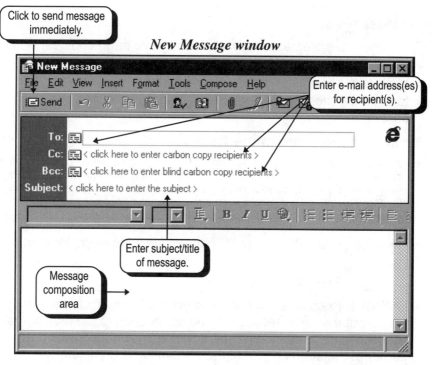

New Message window

- After inserting the address(es) in the To field, you may click in either of the following fields and enter the recipient information indicated.

| **CC (Carbon Copy)** | The e-mail addresses of people who will receive copies of the message. |
| **BCC (Blind Carbon Copy)** | Same as CC, except these names will not appear anywhere in the message, so other recipients will not know that the person(s) listed in the BCC field received a copy. |

- Click in the Subject field and type the subject of the message. An entry in this field is required.

- Click in the blank composition area below the Subject field and type the body of your message. Wordwrap occurs automatically, and you can cut and paste quotes from other messages or text from other programs. You can also check the spelling of your message by selecting Spelling from the Tools menu and responding to the prompts that follow.

Send Messages

- Once you have created a message, you have three choices:
  - to send the message immediately
  - to store the message in the Outbox folder to be sent later
  - to save the message in the Drafts folder to be edited and sent later

To send a message immediately:

√ *To be able to send messages immediately, you must first select Options from the Tools menu in the Mail window. Then click on the Send tab and select the Send messages immediately check box. If this option is not selected, clicking the Send button will not send a message immediately, but will send the message to your Outbox until you perform the Send and Receive task.*

- Click the send button ⌐🖃 Send⌐ on the New Message toolbar.

  OR

  Click File, Send Message.

- Outlook Express then connects to your ISP's mail server and sends out the new message. If the connection to the mail server is successful, the sending mail icon displays in the lower-right corner of the status bar until the transmittal is complete:

- Sometimes, however, Outlook Express cannot immediately connect to the mail server and instead has to store the new message in the Outbox for later delivery. When this happens, the sending mail icon does not appear, and the number next to your Outbox folder increases by one ⌐🖃 Outbox (1)⌐.

- Outlook Express does not automatically reattempt to send a message after a failed connection. Instead, you need to manually send the message from the Outbox (see "To send messages from your Outbox folder" on page 57).

To store a message in your Outbox folder for later delivery:

- Select File, Send Later in the New Message window.

- The Send Mail prompt displays, telling you that the message will be stored in our Outbox folder.

- Click OK.

- The message is saved in the Outbox.

56

To send messages from your Outbox folder:

- Click on the Send and Receive button 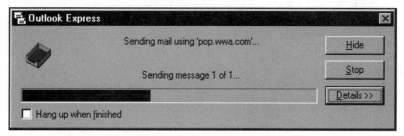 on the toolbar.
  OR
- Click Tools, Send and Receive, All Accounts.

√ *When you use the Send and Receive command, Outlook Express sends out* **all** *messages stored in the Outbox and automatically downloads any new mail messages from the mail server.*

- After you click Send and Receive, a dialog box opens, displaying the status of the transmittal.

To save a message to your Drafts folder:

- Click File, Save.
- The Saved Message prompt displays. Click OK.

To edit and send message drafts:

- In the Mail window, click in the Drafts folder  from the Mail Folder list.
- Double-click on the desired message header from the message list.
- In the New Message window that appears, edit your message as necessary. When you are finished, select File, Send Message to

send the message immediately, or Eile, Send Later to store it in the Outbox folder for later delivery.

■ Outlook Express automatically saves all sent messages in the Sent Items folder. To view a list of the messages you have sent, select the Sent Items folder ⎡ ⟨🖻 Sent Items⎤ from the Mail Folder list. The contents will display in the message list pane.

Reply to Mail

■ In Outlook Express, you can reply to a message automatically, without having to enter the recipient's name or e-mail address.

■ When replying, you have a choice of replying to the author and all recipients of the original message or to the author only.

■ To reply to the author and all recipients:

• Select the message you want to reply to from the message list in the Mail window.

• Click the Reply to All button ⎡Reply to All⎤ on the Mail toolbar.

  OR

• Right-click on the selected message and select Reply to All.

■ To reply to the author only:

• Click the Reply to Author button ⎡Reply to Author⎤ on the Mail toolbar.

  OR

• Right-click on the selected message and select Reply to Author.

■ Once you have selected a reply command, the New Message window opens with the address fields and the Subject filled in for you.

√ *You can access all of the mail send commands by right-clicking on the message in the Message list.*

- The original message is automatically included in the body of your response. To turn off this default insertion, select Options from the Tools menu, click on the Send tab, deselect the Include message in reply check box, and click OK.

- To compose your reply, click in the composition area and type your text as you would in a new message.

- When you are done, click the Send button [Send] on the New Message toolbar to send the message immediately. Or, select Send Later from the File menu to store the message in the Outbox folder for later delivery. To save the reply as a draft to be edited and sent later, select Save from the File menu.

Forward Mail

- To forward a message automatically without having to enter the message subject:

  - Select the message to forward from the message list in the Mail window.

  - Click the Forward Message button [Forward Message] on the Mail toolbar.

    The New Message window opens with the original message displayed and the Subject field filled in for you.

- Fill in the e-mail address information by either typing each address or selecting the recipients from your address book. (See "Address a New Message Using the Personal Address Book" on page 62.)

  √ *If you are forwarding the message to multiple recipients, insert a comma or semicolon between each recipient's address.*

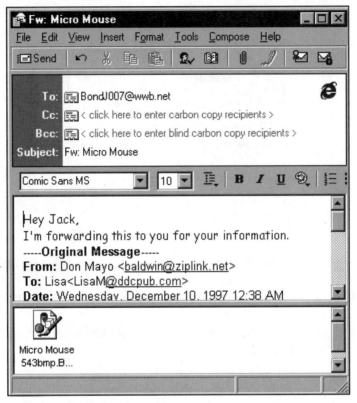

- Click in the composition area and type any text you wish to send with the forwarded message.

- When you are done, click the Send button ⌐∃Send on the New Message toolbar to send the message immediately. Or, select Send Later from the File menu to store the message in the Outbox folder for later delivery. To save the reply as a draft to be edited and sent later, select Save from the File menu.

Add Entries to the Personal Address Book

- In Outlook Express, you can use the Windows Address Book to store e-mail addresses and other information about your most common e-mail recipients. You can then use the Address Book to find and automatically insert addresses when creating new messages.

- To open the Windows Address Book:

  - Click the Address Book button on the toolbar in the Mail window or the Main window.

The Address Book window opens, displaying a list of contacts.

Address Book Window

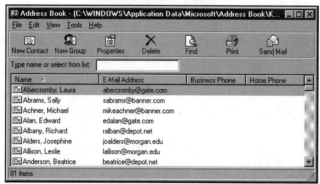

- To add a name to the address book:

  - Click the New Contact button ![New Contact] on the Address Book toolbar.

  - In the Properties dialog box that displays, type the First, Middle and Last names of the new contact in the appropriate text boxes.

  - Type the contact's e-mail address in the Add new text box and then click the Add button. You can repeat this procedure if you wish to list additional e-mail addresses for the contact.

  - In the Nickname text box, you can enter a nickname for the contact (the nickname must be unique among the entries in your address book). When addressing a new message, you can type the nickname in the To field, rather than typing the entire address, and Outlook Express will automatically complete the address.

Contact Properties Dialog Box

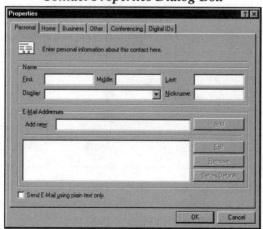

- You can automatically add the name and address of the sender of a message by opening the message in the Message window, right-clicking on the sender's name in the To field, and selecting Add to Address Book from the shortcut menu.

- You can also set Outlook Express to add the address of recipients automatically when you reply to a message. To do so, select Options from the Tools menu and select the Automatically put people I reply to in my Address Book check box on the General tab.

- You can edit an Address Book entry at any time by double-clicking on the person's name in the contact list in the Address Book window.

Address a New Message Using the Personal Address Book

- To insert an address from your address book into a new message:

  - Click the Select Recipients button 📖 on the New Message toolbar.

  - In the Select Recipients dialog box that follows, select the address to insert from the contact list.

Select Recipients Dialog Box

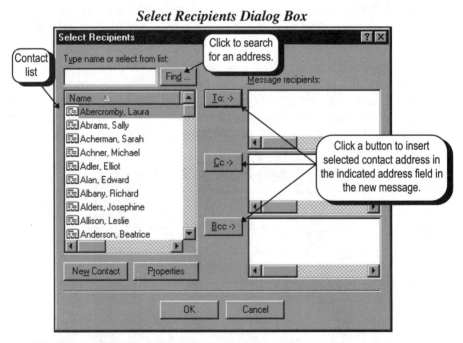

  - Click the button for the field in which you want to insert the address (To, Cc, or Bcc). Click OK to return to the New Message window when you are finished.

Outlook Express: 12

◆ **View Attached Files** ◆ **Save Attached Files** ◆ **Attach Files to a Message**

View Attached Files

- Sometimes an e-mail message will come with a separate file(s) attached. Messages containing attachments are indicated in the message list in the Mail window by a paperclip icon 📎 to the left of the message header.

- If the selected message is displayed in the preview pane, a larger paper clip attachment icon will appear to the right of the header at the top of the preview pane.

Mail Window

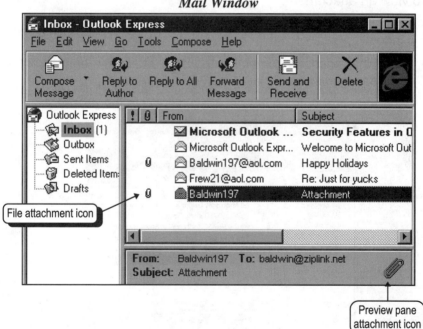

- If you open the selected message in its own window, an attachment icon will appear in a separate pane below the message.

- To view an attachment:
  - Open the folder containing the desired message in the Mail window.
  - Select the message containing the desired attachment(s) from the message list to display it in the preview pane.

    If the attachment is an image, it will display in the message.

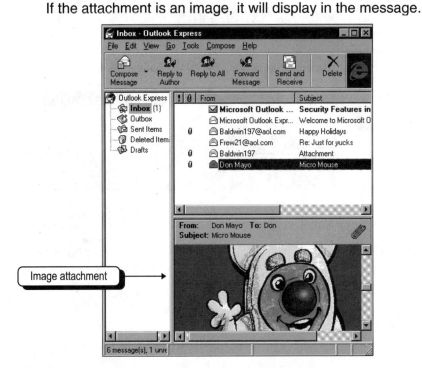

√ *If the image does not display, click Tools, Options, click the Read tab, select the Automatically show picture attachments in messages check box, and click OK.*

- Other types of attachments, such as a program, word processor document, or media clip, do not display in the message, but have to be opened in a separate window. To do so:

  - Click on the attachment icon 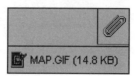 in the preview pane. A button will display with the file name and size of the attachment.

    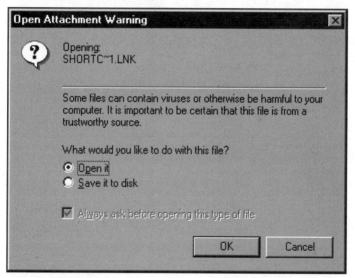

  - Click on this button.

  - If the Open Attachment Warning dialog box displays, select the Open it option and click OK.

- Outlook Express will open the attached file or play the attached media clip.

- If the attached file does not open, Outlook Express does not recognize the file type of the attached file (that is, Outlook Express does not contain the plug-in, or your computer does not contain the application needed to view it).

- To view an unrecognized attachment, you have to install and/or open the application or plug-in needed to view it.

Save Attached Files

■ If desired, you can save an attached file to your hard drive or disk for future use or reference. To save an attachment:

• Select Save Attachments from the File menu, and select the attachment to save from the submenu that displays.

OR

• Right-click on the attachment icon 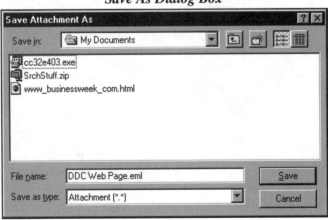 in the Message window and select the Save As option.

• In the Save As dialog box that follows, click the Save in drop-down list box and select the drive and folder in which to save the file.

Save As Dialog Box

• Click in the File name text box and type a name for the file.
• Click Save.

Attach Files to a Message

■ You can attach a file to an e-mail message while composing the message in the New Message window. To add an attachment:

- Click the Attachments button 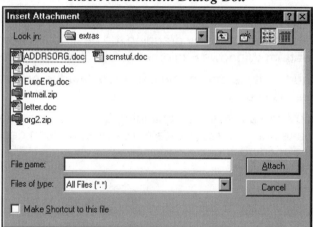 on the New Message toolbar.
  OR
- Click Insert, File Attachment.
- In the Insert Attachment dialog box that appears, click the Look in drop-down list box and select the drive and folder containing the file to attach. Then select the file and click Attach.

Insert Attachment Dialog Box

√ *The attachment will appear as an icon in the body of the message.*

√ *Messages containing attachments usually take longer to send than those without attachments.*

√ *When attaching very large files or multiple files, you may want to zip (compress) the files before attaching them. To do so, both you and the recipient need a file compression program, such as WinZip or PKZip.*

New Message Dialog Box

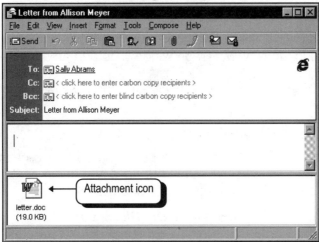

- You can also attach a file by dragging the desired file from your desktop or from Windows Explorer into the New Message window.

- You can add multiple attachments by repeating the procedure as many times as you like.

- Before you send a message containing an attachment, you may wish to make sure the recipient's e-mail program can decode the file you are sending.

America Online: 13

About America Online?

- America Online (AOL) is an all-purpose online service. Unlike Netscape Navigator or Microsoft Internet Explorer, AOL is not an Internet browser, yet you can browse the Internet using AOL navigation features.

- Unlike Internet browsers, AOL does not require a separate Internet Service provider for Internet access, nor does it require a separate mail server connection to access e-mail from the AOL Mail Center. When you install AOL, you configure the program to establish a dial-up connection to the AOL server using your modem. All connections to the Internet and the Mail Center are made via the AOL server.

  √ *An Internet service provider is a company that provides Internet access.*

Start America Online

- To start America Online (Windows 95):

  - Click the AOL icon [America Online 3.0 for Wind...] on your desktop. This icon should display on your desktop after you install AOL.

  OR

  Click the Start button [Start], Programs, America Online, America Online for Windows 95.

  - Make sure your screen name is displayed in the Select Screen Name box and type in your password in the Enter Password box.

  - Click the Sign On button [SIGN ON] to connect to the AOL server.

The AOL Home Page, Menu, and Toolbar

- After you successfully log on to America Online, you will see a series of screens. The final first screen you see is the AOL home page or start page. The AOL home page contains links to daily AOL featured areas as well as links to constant AOL areas such as *Channels* and *What's New*. You can also access your mailbox from the home page.

Home Screen Menu

- The AOL menu displays options currently available. Click the heading to display a drop-down menu of links to AOL areas and basic filing, editing, and display options.

America Online Toolbar

- The AOL toolbar contains buttons for AOL's most commonly used commands. Choosing a button activates the indicated task immediately.

	You have new mail if the flag on the mailbox is in the up position. Click to display a list of new mail in your mailbox.
	Compose and Send Mail Messages. Displays the Composition screen for composing new mail messages.

70

	Channels are areas of interest arranged by category. AOLs 21 channels offer hundreds of AOL areas and Web site connections.
	New and exciting AOL areas to explore including new AOL features, areas, and special interest sites.
	People Connection takes you to the AOL chat area. Here you can access the AOL Community Center, Chat Rooms, and meet the stars in the Live chat forum.
	File Search opens the search window to the software library where you can download hundreds of software programs.
	Stocks and Portfolios links you to the latest stock market quotes, research a company or mutual fund, or find the latest financial news.
	This area not only brings you the latest headline news, weather, and sports but also allows you to search news archives by keywords. You can also see multimedia (slide show and audio) presentations of the hottest topics in the news.
	Connects you to the Web.
	Shop Online in the AOL Marketplace. Goods and services are categorized for your convenience.
	Lets you customize AOL to suit your needs. Each member area shows you step-by-step how to access and select options.
	Click to see an estimate of how long you have been online for the current session.
	Click to print whatever is displayed on your computer screen. Opens the Print dialog box where you can select from the standard print options.
	The Personal Filing Cabinet is a storage area located on your hard disk used to organize files such as downloaded e-mail messages, files, and newsgroup messages.
	Click this icon to create links or shortcuts to your favorite Web sites or AOL areas.
	This is a quick way to access the AOL member directory and to find answers to questions.
	Displays an area called Find Central. Go here to search the AOL directory using keywords and phrases.
	Each AOL area has a keyword to identify the area. Enter the Keyword for immediate access to the desired AOL area.

AOL Help

■ AOL offers extensive Help so that you can learn to use AOL effectively and find answers to any questions you may have about either AOL or the Web. All AOL topics can be printed or saved to your hard disk.

■ To access Help, click Help and the help topic of choice from the menu.

Exit AOL

■ To exit AOL, click the close window button ⊠ in the upper-right corner of the AOL screen.

OR

Click Sign Off, Sign Off on the menu bar.

OR

Click File, Exit.

◆ **Access the Internet from AOL** ◆ **Open a Wold Wide Web Site**
◆ **The AOL Browser Screen** ◆ **Stop a Load or Search**

Access the Internet from AOL

■ To go to the Internet Connection:

- Click the Internet button 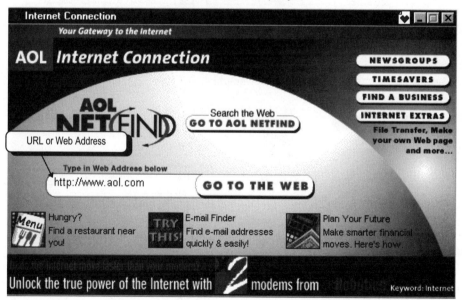 on the AOL main screen.
  OR
- Click **internet** from the Channels menu.
  OR
- Press Ctrl+K, type internet in the Keyword box and press Enter.
  The Internet Connection window displays.

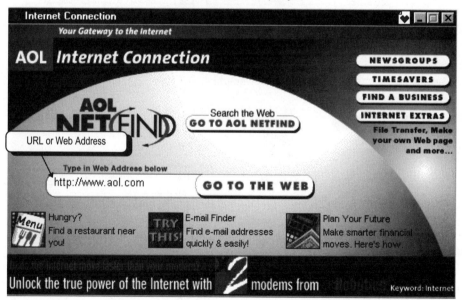

Open a World Wide Web Site

- If you know the Web address (URL), type it into the Type in Web Address below box and click the GO TO THE WEB button **(GO TO THE WEB)** or press Enter. If the Web address is correct, you will be connected to the Web site.

- If you wish to search the Internet, click the GO TO AOL NETFIND button **(GO TO AOL NETFIND)**.
  Search the Web

The AOL Browser Screen

- Once you are connected to the Web, the screen elements change, and the Browser toolbar displays.

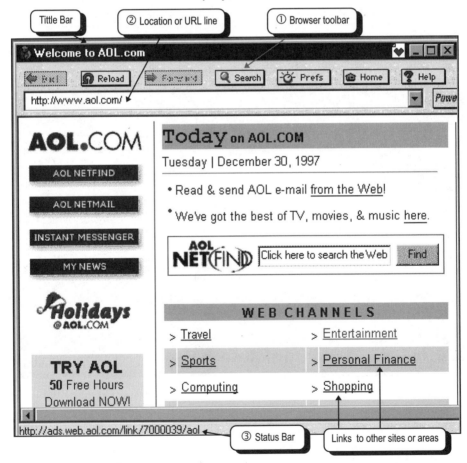

① Browser Toolbar

- The AOL Browser toolbar will help you navigate through sites you visit on the Web. Buttons on the Browser toolbar also connect you to search and Internet preference areas.

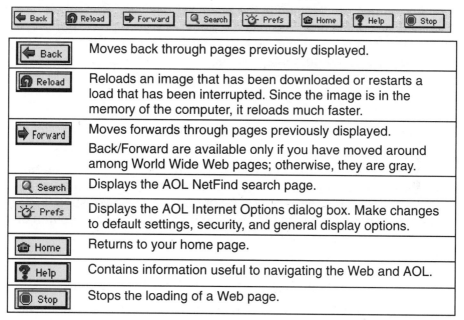

Back	Moves back through pages previously displayed.
Reload	Reloads an image that has been downloaded or restarts a load that has been interrupted. Since the image is in the memory of the computer, it reloads much faster.
Forward	Moves forwards through pages previously displayed. Back/Forward are available only if you have moved around among World Wide Web pages; otherwise, they are gray.
Search	Displays the AOL NetFind search page.
Prefs	Displays the AOL Internet Options dialog box. Make changes to default settings, security, and general display options.
Home	Returns to your home page.
Help	Contains information useful to navigating the Web and AOL.
Stop	Stops the loading of a Web page.

② Location Line

- AOL stores each Web address you visit during each AOL session. If you wish to return to an address you have visited during the current session, you can click the location box arrow and click the address from the pull-down list.

③ Status Bar

- The Status bar, located at the bottom of the screen, is a helpful indicator of the progress of the loading of a Web page. For example, if you are loading a Web site, you will see the byte size of the page, the percentage of the task completed, and the number of graphics and links yet to load. In many cases the time it will take to load the page will display.

Stop a Load or Search

- Searching for information or loading a Web page can be time-consuming, especially if the Web page has many graphic images, if a large number of people are trying to access the site at the same time, or if your modem and computer operate at slower speeds. If data is taking a long time to load, you may wish to stop a search or the loading of a page or large file.

- To stop a search or load:

  - Click the Stop button [⬤ Stop] on the Navigation toolbar.

- If you decide to continue the load after clicking the Stop button, click the Reload button [↻ Reload].

◆ Favorite Places ◆ Add Favorite Places ◆ View Favorite Places
◆ Delete Favorite Places ◆ AOL History List
◆ Save Web Pages ◆ Print Web Pages

Favorite Places

- A **Favorite Place** listing is a bookmark that you create containing the title, URL, and a direct link to a Web page or AOL area that you may want to revisit. A Favorite Place listings links directly to the desired page.

- The AOL Favorite Place feature allows you to maintain a record of Web sites in your Favorite Places file so that you can return to them easily. (See "Add Favorite Places" below.)

Add Favorite Places

- There are several ways to mark an AOL area or Web site and save it as a Favorite Place. Once the page is displayed:

  - Click the Favorite Place heart 💟 on the Web site or AOL area title bar.

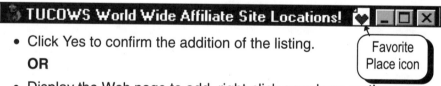

  - Click Yes to confirm the addition of the listing.

    Favorite Place icon

  OR

  - Display the Web page to add, right-click anywhere on the page and select Add to Favorites from the shortcut menu.

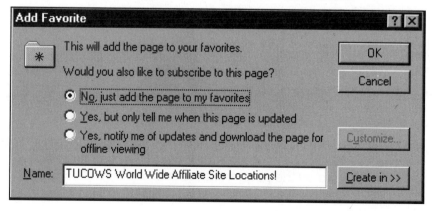

- Click the desired option from the confirmation box that displays and click OK.
- The site will automatically be added to your Favorite Places list.

View Favorite Places

■ You can view the Favorite Places file by selecting <u>Go To</u>, Favorite

Places, or by clicking on the Favorite Places button on the AOL toolbar. Click on any listing from the list to go directly to that page.

■ The details of any Favorite Place listing can be viewed or modified by using the buttons on the Favorite Places screen.

Delete Favorite Places

■ You may wish to delete a Favorite Place if a Web site no longer exists or remove an AOL area from the listing that is no longer of interest to you.

To delete a Favorite Place:

- Click the Favorite Places button on the toolbar.
- Click on the listing to delete.
- Click the Delete button **Delete** from the Favorite Places screen.
  OR
- Right-click on the listing and select Delete from the pop-up menu.
  OR
- Press the Delete key.
- Click YES to confirm the deletion.

AOL History List

■ While you move back and forth within a Web site, AOL automatically records each page location. The history is only temporary and is deleted when you sign-off. AOL areas are not recorded in the history list.

■ To view the history list, click on the arrow at the end of the URL line. You can use History to jump back or forward to recently viewed pages by clicking on the page from the list.

78

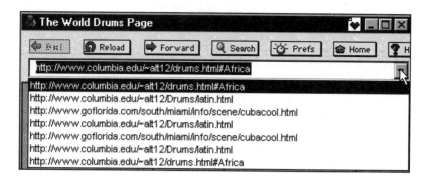

Save Web Pages

- When you find a Web page with information that you would like to keep for future reference, or to review later offline, you can save it to your hard disk. To save a Web page:

  - Click File, Save

  - Type a filename in the File name box.

    √ *When you save a Web page, often the current page name appears in the File name box. You can use this name or type a new one.*

  - Choose the drive and folder in which to store the file from the Save in drop-down list

  - Click Save.

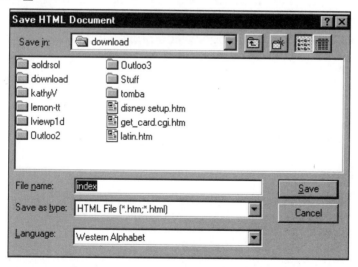

- In most cases when you choose to save a Web page, AOL will automatically save it as an HTML file. Saving a page as an HTML file saves the original formatting and, when accessed, will display as you saw it on the Web.

- You can also save a Web page as a Plain text file which saves only the page text without the formatting or images and placeholders. You might want to do this when saving a very large file, such as a literary work or multiple-page article. To save in Plain text format, click the down arrow next to the Save as type box in the Save As dialog box and select Plain text from the list.

- You can view a saved Web page later by clicking File, Open, and entering the name and location from the Open a File box or by choosing the location and double-clicking on the file name.

Print Web Pages

- One of the many uses of the Internet is to find and print information. You can print a page as it appears on screen, or you can print it as plain text. Only displayed pages can be printed. To print a Web page, display it and do the following:

    • Click the Print button on the AOL toolbar.

    OR

    • Click Print on the File menu.

    • In the Print dialog box that displays, select the desired print options and click OK.

- In most cases, the Web page will be printed in the format shown in the Web page display.

America Online E-mail: 16

◆ Read New Mail ◆ Compose a New Mail Message
◆ Send Messages ◆ Reply to Mail
◆ Forward Mail ◆ AOL Mail Help

Read New Mail

■ There are several ways to know whether you have new mail in your mailbox: If your computer has a sound card and speakers, you will hear "You've Got Mail" when you successfully connect to AOL. The link is replaced by the You Have Mail link, and the mailbox icon on the main screen has the flag in the up position .

To display and read new and unread mail:

- Click the You Have Mail button on the AOL main screen.
  OR
- Click the Read New Mail button [icon] on the main screen toolbar
  OR
- Press Ctrl+R.

  √ *The New Mail list displays new and unread mail for the screen name used for this session. If you have more than one screen name, you must sign on under each name to retrieve new mail.*

  √ *New and Unread e-mail messages remain on the AOL mail server for approximately 27 days before being deleted by AOL. If you want to save a message to your hard disk, click File, Save As and choose a location for the message. By default the message will be saved to the Download folder.*

- To read a message, double-click on it from the New Mail list.

Compose a New Mail Message

- Click Mail, Compose Mail.
  OR
- Click the Compose Mail button [icon] on the main screen toolbar.
  OR
- Click Ctrl+M.

The Compose Mail screen displays.

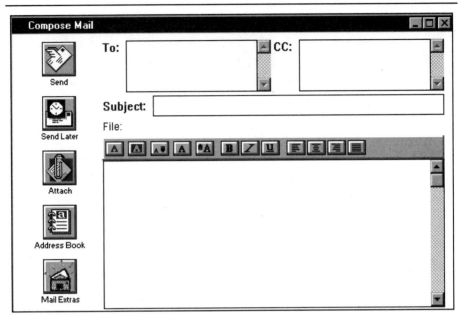

- Fill in the e-mail address(es) in the To box of the Compose Mail screen.

  OR

- Select Address Book and double-click to select an address. (See "America Online E-mail: 18" on page 88 for more information on your Address book.)

- If you are sending the same message to multiple recipients, fill in the CC: (Carbon Copy) box with the e-mail addresses of recipients who will receive a copy of this message. These names will display to all recipients of the message.

- If you want to send BCC: (Blind courtesy copies—copies of a message sent to others but whose names are not visible to the main or other recipients), put the address in parenthesis, for example: (ddcpub.com).

  √ *Multiple addresses must be separated with a comma.*

- Fill in the Subject box with a one-line summary of your message. AOL will not deliver a message without a subject heading. This is the first thing the recipient sees in the list of new mail when your message is delivered.

- Fill in the body of the message.

Send Messages

- Click the Send button [Send] to send the message immediately. *You must be online.*

  OR

- Click the Send Later button [Send Later] to send a message later that you have composed offline.

Reply to Mail

- You can reply to mail messages while online or compose replies to e-mail offline to send later.

- To reply to e-mail:

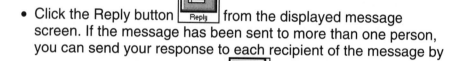

- Click the Reply button [Reply] from the displayed message screen. If the message has been sent to more than one person, you can send your response to each recipient of the message by

  clicking the Reply to All button [Reply to All]. The addresses of the sender and, if desired, all recipients will be automatically inserted into the address fields.

  √ *To include part or all of the original message in your Reply, select the contents of the original message to be included in quotes in your message and click the Reply button to begin your reply.*

- Click the Send button [Send] if you are online and want to send

  the reply immediately or click the Send Later button [Send Later].

Forward Mail

- There are times when you may want to send mail sent to you on to someone else.

- To forward e-mail:

  - Click the Forward button [Forward] from the displayed message screen and fill in the address(es) of the recipients of the forwarded message. The Subject heading from the original message is automatically inserted into the subject heading box.

  - Click the Send button [Send] if you are online and want to send the reply immediately or click the Send Later button [Send Later].

AOL Mail Help

- For answers to many of your basic e-mail questions, click Mail, Mail Center, and click on the Let's Get Started button [LET'S GET STARTED!].

◆ **Add Attachments to a Message**
◆ **Download File Attachments**

Add Attachments to a Message

■ You can attach a file to send along with any e-mail message. Before you send a file attachment—especially if it is a multimedia file—it is a good idea to make sure that the recipient's e-mail program can read the attachment. For example, files sent in MIME format cannot be viewed by AOL e-mail and require separate software to be opened.

To attach files to a message:

• Compose the message to be sent. (See "Compose a New Mail Message" on page 81.)

• Click the Attach button ⌷Attach⌷ on the Compose Message screen.

• Select the drive and folder where the file you wish to attach is located.

• Double-click the file to attach from the Attach File dialog box.
   √ *The attachment will appear below the Subject box.*

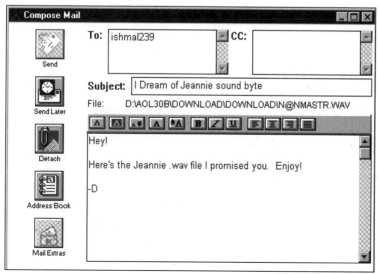

- If you are online, click the Send button ![Send] to send the

  message immediately, or click the Send Later button ![Send Later] to store the message in your Outgoing Mail if you are working offline.

  √ *Multiple files must be grouped together in a single archive using a file compression program such as PKZIP or WINZIP. Both you and the recipient will need a file compression program.*

Download E-mail File Attachments

- An e-mail message that arrives with a file attachment is displayed in your new mail list with a small diskette under the message icon.

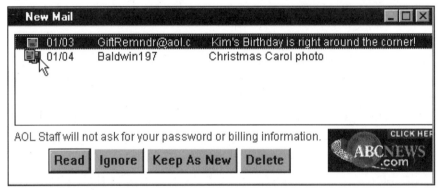

- Opening the message and viewing the attachment are two separate steps:

  - Open the message by double-clicking on it from the New Mail list (see "To display and read new and unread mail" on page 81). The message will display.

  - You can choose to download the file attachment immediately by clicking the Download File button ![Download File] at the bottom of the displayed message screen. Click the Save button ![Save] on the Download Manager screen to save the file, by default, to the AOL30/Download folder. If you desire, you can change the save destination folder.

- A status box will display while the attachment is being downloaded or transferred to your computer.

- At the end of the download, the file transfer box will close and you will see the message "File's Done."

OR

- You may choose to download the file later. Click the Download Later button **Download Later** to store the message in the Download Manager. When you are ready to download the file, click File, Download Manager, and then select the file to download. You must be online.

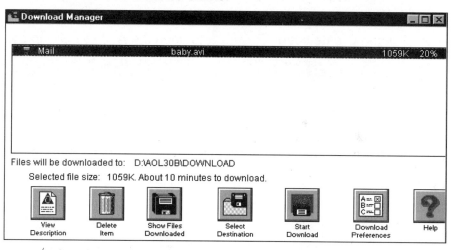

√ *Click Sign off after transfer if you want AOL to automatically disconnect when the transfer is complete.*

To change the default location of where files are stored:

- Click the Select Destination button from the Download Manager screen and choose the desired destination from the Select Path dialog box.

◆ **Add Entries to the Address Book**
◆ **Enter an Address Using the Address Book**

Add Entries to the Address Book

■ Once you start sending e-mail, you may be surprised at how many people you start to communicate with online. An easy way to keep track of e-mail addresses is to enter them into the Address Book. Once an e-mail address entry has been created, you can automatically insert it from the Address Book into the address fields.

To create Address Book entries:

• Click <u>M</u>ail, Edit <u>A</u>ddress Book. The Address Book dialog box displays.

• Click the Create button [Create] to open the Address Group box.

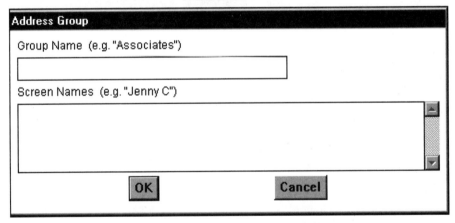

• Enter the real name or nickname of the e-mail recipient (e.g., JohnV) or the name of a Group listing (e.g., Book Club) in the Group Name box. The name you enter in this box is the name that will appear in the Address Book list.

• Press the Tab key to move to the Screen Names box and enter the complete e-mail address of the recipient or the e-mail addresses of everyone in the group listing. When entering multiple addresses such as in a group listing, each address must be separated by a comma (e.g., Baldwin168, BubbaB@ziplink.net, etc.).

- Click OK.

  √ *When sending mail to AOL members through AOL, you do not need to enter the @aol.com domain information. Enter only their screen name as the e-mail address. For all other Address Book entries you must enter the entire address.*

Delete an Address Book Entry

- Click Mail, Edit Address Book to open the Address Book.
- Click the name to delete.
- Click the Delete button Delete .
- Click Yes.
- Click OK to close the Address Book.

Enter an Address Using the Address Book

- Place the cursor in the desired address field.

- Click the Address Book button Address Book to open the Address Book.
- Double-click the name or names from the Address Book list to insert in the TO: or CC: address box and click OK.

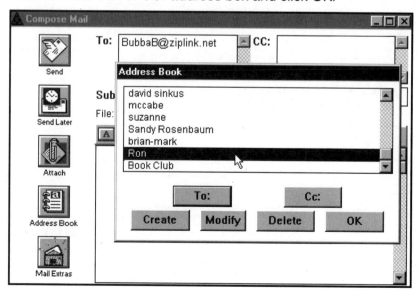

◆ **Searching vs. Surfing** ◆ **Search Sites** ◆ **Search Basics**

Searching vs. Surfing

■ The Web is a vast source of information, but to find information that you want, you must be able to locate it. The Web has many thousands of locations, containing hundreds of thousands of pages of information.

■ Unlike libraries that use either the Library of Congress or Dewey Decimal system to catalog information, the Internet has no uniform way of tracking and indexing information. You can find lots of information on the Internet; the trick is to find information that you want. Initially, it may seem easy to find information on the Web— you just connect to a relevant site and then start clicking on links to related sites. Illustrated below is an example of a search that starts out on one topic and ends on an unrelated one.

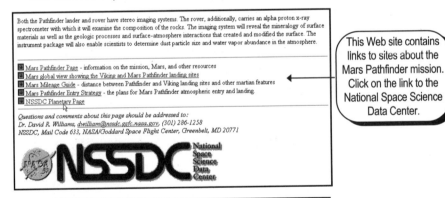

Upcoming Planetary Events and Missions

Upcoming Planetary Launches and Events

1997 December 16 - <u>Galileo</u> - Europa closest flyby

1998 January 6 - <u>Lunar Prospector</u> - Launch of NASA Global Orbiter Mission to the Moon
1998 January 23 - <u>NEAR</u> - Earth Flyby
1998 April 26 - <u>Cassini</u> - Venus-1 Flyby
1998 July - <u>New Millenium Deep Space-1</u> - Launch of NASA Flyby Mission to Asteroid 3352 McAuliffe and Comet
P/West-Kohoutek-Ikemura
1998 August 6 - <u>Planet-B</u> - Launch of ISAS (Japan) Orbiter Mission to Mars
1998 December - <u>Mars Surveyor '98 Orbiter</u> - Launch of NASA Orbiter Mission to Mars

> Click on Cassini link to go to a Web site that deals with a project to explore Saturn.

Cassini

Cassini has launched!

Launch Date/Time: 15 October 1997 at 08:43 UTC
Launch Vehicle: Titan IV-Centaur
Planned on-orbit mass: 2175 Kg
Power System: Radioisotope Thermal Generators (RTGs) of 630 W

The Cassini Orbiter's mission consists of delivering a probe (called <u>Huygens</u>, provided by ESA) to Titan, and then remaining in orbit around Saturn for detailed studies of the planet and its rings and satellites. The principal objectives are to: (1) determine the three-dimensional structure and dynamical behavior of the rings; (2) determine the composition of the satellite surfaces and

- This is the stream of consciousness method of searching the Internet (**surfing**). It may be interesting and fun to locate information this way, but there are drawbacks. Surfing randomly for information is time consuming and the results are frequently inconsistent and incomplete. It can also be expensive if you are charged fees for connect time to your Internet Service Provider.

- If you want a more systematic and organized way of looking for information, you can connect to one of several search sites that use **search engines** to track, catalog, and index information on the Internet.

Search Sites

- A **search site** builds its catalog using a search engine. A search engine is a software program that goes out on the Web, seeking Web sites, and cataloging them, usually by downloading their home pages.

- Search sites are classified by the way they gather Web site information. All search sites use a search engine in one way or another to gather information. Below is an explanation of how the major search services assemble and index information.

Search Engines

- A search site builds its catalog using a **search engine**. A search engine is a software program that goes out on the Web, seeking Web sites, and cataloging them, usually by downloading their home pages.

- Search engines are sometimes called **spiders** or **crawlers** because they crawl the Web.

- Search engines constantly visit sites on the Web to create catalogs of Web pages and keep them up to date.

- Major search engines include: **AltaVista**, **HotBot**, **Open Text**.

Directories

- Search **directories** catalog information by building hierarchical indexes. Since humans assemble the catalogs, information is often more relevant than the indexes that are assembled by Web crawlers. Directories may be better organized than search engine sites, but they will not be as complete or up-to-date as search engines that constantly check for new material on the Internet.

- **Yahoo**, the oldest search service on the World Wide Web, is the best example of Internet search directories. Other major search directories are: **Infoseek**, **Magellan**, **Lycos**.

Multi-Threaded Search Engines

- Another type of search engine, called a **multi-threaded** search engine, searches other Web search sites and gathers the results of these searches for your use.

- Because they search the catalogs of other search sites, multi-threaded search sites do not maintain their own catalogs. These search sites provide more search options than subject-and-keyword search sites, and they typically return more specific information with further precision. However, multi-threaded search sites are much slower to return search results than subject-and-keyword search sites.

- Multi-threaded search sites include **SavvySearch** and **Internet Sleuth**.

■ If you are using Internet Explorer or Netscape Navigator, you can click on the Search button on the toolbar to access a number of search services.

Search Basics

■ When you connect to a search site, the home page has a text box for typing the words you want to use in your search. These words are called a **text string**. The text string may be a single word or phrase, or it may be a complex string which uses **operators** to modify the search (see "Search Engines: 21" for more information on operators). Illustrated below is the opening page of Yahoo, one of the oldest and most popular search directories.

Click to initiate search.

Yahoo! Mail
free email

Shop and Win @ NetBuyer

Win a Sports Dream Trip

Links to Yahoo categories

Search options

Yellow Pages - People Search - Maps - Classifieds - Personals - Chat - **Email**
Holiday Shopping - My Yahoo! - News - Sports - Weather - Stoc

Access options to refine search.

- **Arts and Humanities**
  Architecture, Photography, Literature...

- **Business and Economy** [Xtra!]
  Companies, Finance, Employment...

- **Computers and Internet** [Xtra!]
  Internet, WWW, Software, Multimedia...

- **Education**
  Universities, K-12, College Entrance...

- **Entertainment** [Xtra!]
  Cool Links, Movies, Music, Humor...

- **Government**
  Military, Politics [Xtra!], Law, Taxes...

- **Health** [Xtra!]
  Medicine, Drugs, Diseases, Fitness...

- **News and Media** [
  Current Events, Magazines, TV, Newspapers...

- **Recreation and Sports** [Xtra!]
  Sports, Games, Travel, Autos, Outdoors...

- **Reference**
  Libraries, Dictionaries, Phone Numbers...

- **Regional**
  Countries, Regions, U.S. States...

- **Science**
  CS, Biology, Astronomy, Engineering...

- **Social Science**
  Anthropology, Sociology, Economics...

- **Society and Culture**
  People, Environment, Religion...

Yahooligans! for Kids - Beatrice's Guide - MTV/Yahoo! unfURLed - Yahoo! Internet Life
What's New - Weekly Picks - Today's Web Events
Visa Shopping Guide - Yahoo! Store

Regional links

World Yahoos Australia & NZ - Canada - Denmark - France - Germany - Japan - Korea
Norway - SE Asia - Sweden - UK & Ireland
Yahoo! Metros Atlanta - Austin - Boston - Chicago - Dallas / Fort Worth - Los Angeles
Get Local Miami - Minneapolis / St. Paul - New York - S.F. Bay - Seattle - Wash D.C.

Smart Shopping with **VISA**

How to Suggest a Site - Company Info - Openings at Yahoo! - Contributors - Yahoo! to Go

- Once you have entered a text string, initiate the search by either pressing the Enter key or by clicking on the search button. This button may be called Search, Go Get It, Seek Now, Find, or something similar.
- For the best search results:
  - Always check for misspelled words and typing errors.
  - Use descriptive words and phrases.
  - Use synonyms and variations of words.
  - Find and follow the instructions that the search site suggests for constructing a good search.
  - Eliminate unnecessary words (the, a, an, etc.) from the search string. Concentrate on key words and phrases.
  - Test your search string on several different search sites. Search results from different sites can vary greatly.
  - Explore some of the sites that appear on your initial search and locate terms that would help you refine your search string.

Search Engines: 20

◆ Simple Searches ◆ Refine a Search ◆ Get Help

Simple Searches

■ Searches can be simple or complex, depending on how you design the search string in the text box.

■ A **simple search** uses a text string, usually one or two key words, to search for matches in a search engine's catalog. A simple search is the broadest kind of search.

  • The key words may be specific, such as Internet Explorer browser, current stock quotes, or Macintosh computers, or they may be general, such as software, economy, or computer.

  • The catalog search will return a list, typically quite large, of Web pages and URLs whose descriptions contain the text string you want to find. Frequently these searches will yield results with completely unrelated items.

■ When you start a search, the Web site searches its catalog for occurrences of your text string. (Some search sites don't have their own catalog, so they search the catalogs of other search sites.) The results of the search, typically a list of Web sites whose descriptions have words that match your text string are displayed in the window of your browser.

■ Each search site has its own criteria for rating the matches of a catalog search and setting the order in which they are displayed.

■ The catalog usually searches for matches of the text string in the URLs of Web sites. It also searches for key words, phrases, and meta-tags (key words that are part of the Web page, but are not displayed in a browser) in the cataloged Web pages.

■ The information displayed on the results page will vary, depending on the search and display options selected and the search site you are using. The most likely matches for your text string appear first in the results list, followed by other likely matches on successive pages.

  √ There may be thousands of matches that contain the search string you specified. The matches are displayed a page at a time. You can view the next page by clicking on the "next page" link provided at the bottom of each search results page.

- For example, if you do a search on the word *Greek*, you'll get results, as illustrated below, that display links to a wide range of links that have something to do with Greek. Note the number of documents that contain the search word.

  √ *These examples use AltaVista to perform the search. Your results may vary with other search tools.*

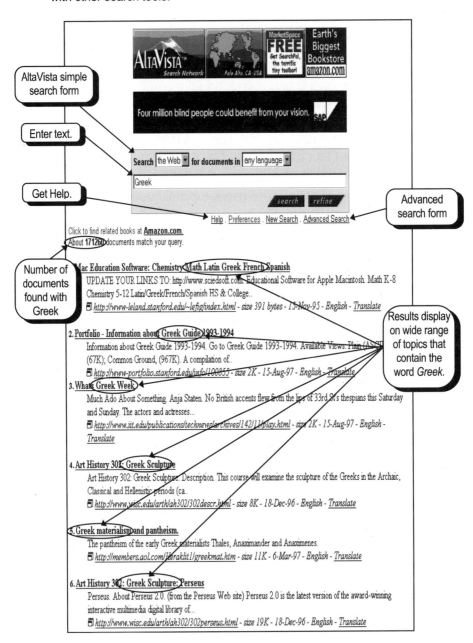

■ You can scan the displayed results to see if a site contains the information you are looking for. Site names are clickable links. After visiting a site, you can return to the search site by clicking the Back button on your browser. You can then choose a different site to visit or perform another search.

Refine a Search

■ Suppose that you only want to view links that deal with Greek *tragedies*. The natural inclination would be to enter Greek tragedies in the search string to reduce the number of documents that the search tool finds. Note, however, the number of documents that were found when Greek tragedies was entered in this search. Since the search string didn't include a special operator to tell the search engine to look for sites that contain both Greek *and* tragedies, the results display sites that contain Greek *OR* tragedies in addition to sites that contain Greek *AND* tragedies.

■ To reduce the number of documents in this search, enter *Greek* press space once, then enter a plus sign (+) and the word tragedies (Greek +tragedies) then click Search. This tells AltaVista to look for articles that contain Greek *and* tragedies in the documents. Note the results that display when the plus is added to the search.

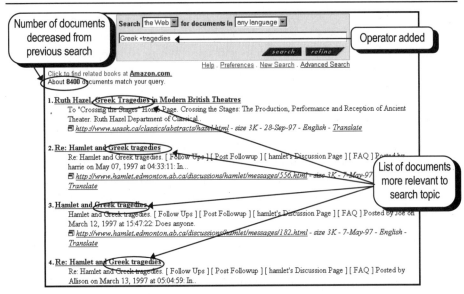

Number of documents decreased from previous search

Search [the Web ▼] for documents in [any language ▼]

Greek +tragedies ◄

Operator added

search *refine*

Help . Preferences . New Search . Advanced Search

Click to find related books at **Amazon.com.**
About **8400** documents match your query.

1. **Ruth Hazel, Greek Tragedies in Modern British Theatres**
   To "Crossing the Stages" Home Page. Crossing the Stages: The Production, Performance and Reception of Ancient Theater. Ruth Hazel Department of Classical..
   http://www.usask.ca/classics/abstracts/hazel.html - size 3K - 28-Sep-97 - English - _Translate_

2. **Re: Hamlet and Greek tragedies**
   Re: Hamlet and Greek tragedies. [Follow Ups] [Post Followup] [hamlet's Discussion Page] [FAQ] Posted by harrie on May 07, 1997 at 04:33:11: In...
   http://www.hamlet.edmonton.ab.ca/discussions/hamlet/messages/556.html - size 3K - 7-May-97 - _Translate_

3. **Hamlet and Greek tragedies**
   Hamlet and Greek tragedies. [Follow Ups] [Post Followup] [hamlet's Discussion Page] [FAQ] Posted by Joe on March 12, 1997 at 15:47:22: Does anyone.
   http://www.hamlet.edmonton.ab.ca/discussions/hamlet/messages/182.html - size 3K - 7-May-97 - English - _Translate_

4. **Re: Hamlet and Greek tragedies**
   Re: Hamlet and Greek tragedies. [Follow Ups] [Post Followup] [hamlet's Discussion Page] [FAQ] Posted by Allison on March 13, 1997 at 05:04:59: In..

List of documents more relevant to search topic

- The number of documents listed is dramatically reduced, and the documents displayed display information that is more closely related to the topic, Greek tragedies.

- You can also *exclude* words by using the minus sign (-) to further refine a search and eliminate unwanted documents in the results. For example, if you wanted to find articles about Greek tragedies but not ones that deal with Hamlet, enter a search string like this: *Greek +tragedies -Hamlet*. Note the different results that display:

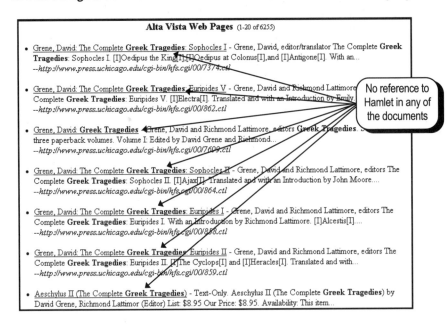

Alta Vista Web Pages (1-20 of 6255)

- Grene, David: The Complete **Greek Tragedies**: Sophocles I - Grene, David, editor/translator The Complete **Greek Tragedies**: Sophocles I. [I]Oedipus the King[I],[I]Oedipus at Colonus[I],and [I]Antigone[I]. With an...
  --*http://www.press.uchicago.edu/cgi-bin/hfs.cgi/00/7374.ctl*

- Grene, David: The Complete **Greek Tragedies**: Euripides V - Grene, David and Richmond Lattimore Complete **Greek Tragedies**: Euripides V. [I]Electra[I]. Translated and with an Introduction by Emily.
  --*http://www.press.uchicago.edu/cgi-bin/hfs.cgi/00/862.ctl*

- Grene, David: **Greek Tragedies** - Grene, David and Richmond Lattimore, editors **Greek Tragedies**. three paperback volumes. Volume I: Edited by David Grene and Richmond...
  --*http://www.press.uchicago.edu/cgi-bin/hfs.cgi/00/7609.ctl*

- Grene, David: The Complete **Greek Tragedies**: Sophocles II - Grene, David and Richmond Lattimore, editors The Complete **Greek Tragedies**: Sophocles II. [I]Ajax[I]. Translated and with an Introduction by John Moore....
  --*http://www.press.uchicago.edu/cgi-bin/hfs.cgi/00/864.ctl*

- Grene, David: The Complete **Greek Tragedies**: Euripides I - Grene, David and Richmond Lattimore, editors The Complete **Greek Tragedies**: Euripides I. With an Introduction by Richmond Lattimore. [I]Alcestis[I]....
  --*http://www.press.uchicago.edu/cgi-bin/hfs.cgi/00/858.ctl*

- Grene, David: The Complete **Greek Tragedies**: Euripides II - Grene, David and Richmond Lattimore, editors The Complete **Greek Tragedies**: Euripides II. [I]The Cyclops[I] and [I]Heracles[I]. Translated and with...
  --*http://www.press.uchicago.edu/cgi-bin/hfs.cgi/00/859.ctl*

- Aeschylus II (The Complete **Greek Tragedies**) - Text-Only. Aeschylus II (The Complete **Greek Tragedies**) by David Grene, Richmond Lattimor (Editor) List: $8.95 Our Price: $8.95. Availability: This item...

No reference to Hamlet in any of the documents

98

Get Help

■ Check the Help features on the search tool that you are using to see what operators are available. Since there are no standards governing the use of operators, search sites can develop their own. Illustrated on the page 99 are samples of the help available for performing a simple search in AltaVista and Yahoo.

AltaVista Help for Simple Searches

HELP Simple Search

Natural Language queries: (always try this first)

Type a word or phrase or a question (for example, **weather Boston** or **what is the weather in Boston?**), then click Search (or press the Enter key). If the information you want from this sort of query isn't on the first couple of pages, try adding a few more specific words.

Requiring/Excluding Words:

Often you will know a word that will be guaranteed to appear in a document for which you are searching. If this is the case, require that the word appear in all of the results by attaching a "+" to the beginning of the word (for example, to find an article on pet care, you might try the query **dog cat pet +care**). You may also find that when you search on a vague topic, you get a very broad set of results. You can quickly reject results by adding a term that appears often in unwanted articles with a "-" before it (for example, to find a recipe for oatmeal raisin cookies without nuts try **oatmeal raisin cookie -nut* -walnut***).

Exact Phrases:

If you know that a certain phrase will appear on the page you are looking for, put the phrase in quotes. (for example, try entering song lyrics such as **"you ain't nothing but a hound dog"**)

Yahoo Help for Simple Searches

Tips for Better Searching

- **Use Double Quotes Around Words that are Part of a Phrase**

  example `"great barrier reef"` [Search]

- **Specify Words that Must Appear in the Results**
  Attach a + in front words that *must* appear in result documents.

  example: `sting +police` [Search]

- **Specify Words that Should Not Appear in the Results**
  Attach a – in front of words that *must not* appear in result documents.

  example: `python -monty` [Search]

Search Engines: 21

Complex Searches

- When you first connect to a search site, the temptation to type in text and hit the search button is great. Resist it. Taking time to read and understand the search rules of the site will save the time you'll waste by creating a search that yields an overwhelming number of hits. Some of what you want may be buried somewhere in that enormous list, but working your way through the irrelevant sites can waste time, cause frustration, and be very discouraging.

- In "Search Engines: 20," you learned how simply using a plus or minus sign can create a search that gives a more pertinent list of sites. Now, you will see how to use operators to restrict and refine your searches even more.

Operators

- A **complex search** usually contains several words in the text string including **operators** that modify the text string. Operators are words or symbols that modify the search string instead of being part of it.

- Using operators and several descriptive words can narrow your search for information, which means the results will reduce the number of sites that display. This means the resulting list of sites should be more relevant to what you want, thereby saving you time and probably money.

- Each search site develops its own set of restrictions and options to create searches designed to locate specific information. What follows are some of the commonly used operators and how they are used.

100

Boolean Operators

- **Boolean operators** specify required words, excluded words, and complex combinations of words to be found during a search. Depending on the site, Boolean operators may be represented by words or symbols.

- The most common Boolean operators are:

AND	The documents found in the search must contain *all words* joined by the AND operator. For example, a search for *Microsoft* AND *Internet* AND *Explorer* will find sites which contain all three words (*Microsoft*, *Internet*, and *Explorer*).
OR	The documents found in the search must contain *at least one of the words* joined by the OR operator. The documents may contain both, but this is not required. For example, a search for *Web* OR *Internet* will find sites which contain either the word *Web* or the word *Internet*.
NOT	The documents found in the search must not contain the word following the NOT operator. For example, a search for *Washington* NOT *DC* will find sites which contain the word *Washington* but none about *Washington DC*.
NEAR	The documents found in the search must contain the words joined by the NEAR operator within a specified number of words, typically ten. For example, *RAM* NEAR memory will find sites with the word *RAM* and the word *memory* within ten words of each other.

- Suppose that you can't remember the name of the earthquake that occurred during the World Series in San Francisco in 1989. If you enter relevant words in the simple search function (using the plus sign) in AltaVista, here's what you get:

Click to find related books at **Amazon.com**
About **18368** documents match your query.

1. San Francisco Earthquakes
San Francisco Earthquake Links. The Ring of Fire/On Shakey Ground - An Earthquake overview. 1906 Earthquake - Before and After Films. 1906 Earthquake...
http://www.exploratorium.edu/earthquake/sf.earthquakes.html - size 2K - 11-Oct-95 - English

2. Why Earthquakes are Inevitable in the San Francisco Bay Area
Latest quake info. Hazards & Preparedness. More about earthquakes. Studying Earthquakes. Whats new. Home. Why Earthquakes are Inevitable in the San...
http://quake.wr.usgs.gov/hazprep/BayAreaInsert/inevitable.html - size 3K - 21-Mar-97 - English

3. Museums Reach Out With Web Catalogs of Collections /WW November 4 1996
Museums Reach Out With Web Catalogs of Collections. By Susan Moran. Earthquakes chase or keep many people away from California. The violent quake of 1989...
http://www.webweek.com/96Nov04/markcomm/arts_sake.html - size 9K - 17-Apr-97 - English

4. $A History of California Earthquakes (1 of 101)
Content Next. A History of California Earthquakes (Image 1 of 101) Earthquakes in the San Francisco Bay Region. Hayward, 1868. Vacaville, 1892. San...

Results do not answer the question.

- The results display several links to articles about earthquakes in the San Francisco area. If you click on one of these, you may find the earthquake you are looking for.

- Now examine the results of a more complex search using the same words, but using some of the advanced search options available in AltaVista. Entering the search string in the advanced search form of AltaVista displays the following:

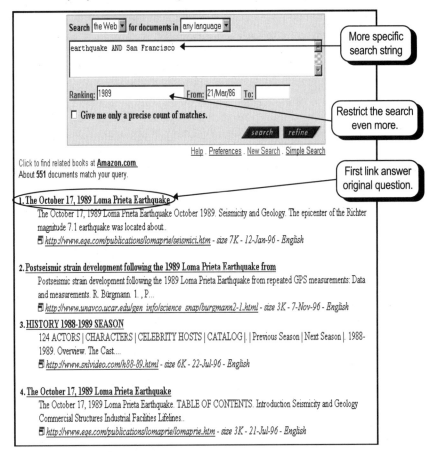

- Use the Advanced search function when you have a specific complex search string; otherwise, use the simple search function. AltaVista will automatically rank the order of the search results when you use the simple search function. When you use the advanced search function, you control the ranking of the results by entering additional search criteria in the Ranking box on the Advanced search form.

Plus (+)/Minus (-) System

- Boolean logic is the basis for the plus and minus system of constructing a search. If the plus/minus sign is not included in the search string, the search engine assumes that you are using OR. That's why when you searched for *Greek tragedies*, AltaVista looked for documents containing either *Greek* or *tragedies*.

Plus sign (+)   Placed immediately in front of a word (no space between the plus sign and the word) means that all documents found must contain that word. (This is similar to the Boolean AND function.) For example, note the results of a search for articles about earthquakes in California, using a search string like this: *earthquakes +California*.

Click to find related books at **Amazon.com.**
About **59247** documents match your query.

1. **$A History of California Earthquakes (5 of 101)**
   Content Previous Next. A History of California Earthquakes (Image 5 of 101) Earthquake damage in San Francisco Bay Region.
   http://www.johnmartin.com/eqshow/cah_0105.htm - size 399 bytes - 5-Dec-96 - English

2. **$A History of California Earthquakes (2 of 101)**
   Content Previous Next. A History of California Earthquakes (Image 2 of 101) State map with major fault systems.
   http://www.johnmartin.com/eqshow/cah_0102.htm - size 389 bytes - 5-Dec-96 - English

3. **Earthquakes in California**
   EARTHQUAKES IN CALIFORNIA. California is the highest earthquake risk area in the contiguous United States. Several large, well-known active faults run...
   http://www.eqe.com/publications/homeprep/eqkesca.htm - size 4K - 26-Nov-95 - English

4. **$A History of California Earthquakes (16 of 101)**
   Content Previous Next. A History of California Earthquakes (Image 16 of 101) Earthquake damage during the 1957 Daly City earthquake.
   http://www.johnmartin.com/eqshow/cah_0116.htm - size 411 bytes - 5-Dec-96 - English

5. **$A History of California Earthquakes (9 of 101)**
   Content Previous Next. A History of California Earthquakes (Image 9 of 101) Earthquake damage during the 1868 Hayward earthquake.
   http://www.johnmartin.com/eqshow/cah_0109.htm - size 407 bytes - 5-Dec-96 - English

---

Minus sign (-)	Place immediately in front of a word (again, no space) means that all documents found will NOT contain that word. (This is the Boolean NOT function.) For example, note the results of search for articles about earthquakes that do *not include* California using a search string like this: *earthquakes -California*.

Click to find related books at **Amazon.com**
12985 documents match your query.

1. **IGS FAQs - Earthquakes**
   Q: I was born and raised in South Bend, Indiana and I remember experiencing a tremor on a Fall Saturday, right about mid-day, sometime between 1968 and...
   http://www.indiana.edu/~igs/faqs/faqquake.html - size 3K - 15-Jul-97 - English

2. **Index of /ftp/ca.earthquakes/1994/**
   Index of /ftp/ca.earthquakes/1994/ Name Last modified Size Description. Parent Directory 30-Jan-97 10:35 - 940106.gif 16-Nov-94 14:18 11K. 940106.ps.Z...
   http://scec.gps.caltech.edu/ftp/ca.earthquakes/1994/ - size 21K - 15-Aug-97 - English

3. **Index of /ftp/ca.earthquakes/1993/**
   Index of /ftp/ca.earthquakes/1993/ Name Last modified Size Description. Parent Directory 30-Jan-97 10:35 - 930107.ps.Z 08-Aug-94 10:17 40K. 930107.txt.Z...
   http://scec.gps.caltech.edu/ftp/ca.earthquakes/1993/ - size 18K - 15-Aug-97 - English

4. **USENET FAQs - sci.geo.earthquakes**
   USENET FAQs. sci.geo.earthquakes. FAQs in this newsgroup. Satellite Imagery FAQ - Pointer.
   http://www.cis.ohio-state.edu/hypertext/faq/usenet-faqs/bygroup/sci/geo/earthquakes/top.html - size 328 bytes - 15-Aug-97 - English

5. **GEOL 240lxg: Earthquakes**
   GEOL 240lxg: Earthquakes. Department: Earth Sciences. Instructor: Sammis, Charles & Teng, Ta-Liang. Semester offered: Fall Spring. Category: Natural...
   http://www.usc.edu/Library/Gede/GEOL240lxg.SammisCharles.html - size 2K - 22-Nov-95 - English

Grouping Operators

- The grouping **operators** join words and phrases together to be treated as a single unit or determine the order in which Boolean operators are applied.

- The most common grouping operators are:

Double quotes	The documents found in the search must contain the words inside double quotes exactly as entered. For example, a search for *"World Wide Web"* will find sites whose descriptions contain the phrase *World Wide Web*, not the individual words separated by other words or the same words uncapitalized.
Parentheses	Words and operators can be grouped to refine searches using parentheses or to define the order in which Boolean operators are applied. For example, a search for (*Internet OR Web*) AND *browser* will find sites whose descriptions contain the words *Internet* and *browser* or *Web* and *browser*. (Note that this is *not* the same search as *Internet* OR *Web AND browser*, which finds sites whose descriptions contain either the word *Internet* or both of the words *Web* and *browser*.)

Case Sensitive

■ If you enter a word using all lowercase (hamlet), some search engines will look for both upper and lower case versions of the word. If you use uppercase in the search (Hamlet), the search engine will locate documents that only use the uppercase version.

Special Characters and Punctuation

■ Special characters and punctuation can also be used to filter results in complex searches. The most widely used character, the asterisk (*) is used when a word in a search can have a number of different forms. Using the asterisk (*) as a wildcard tells the search engine to find documents that contain any form of the word. For example, if you create a search for blue*, note the wide range of documents that show up in the search results.

Click to find related books at **Amazon.com.**
About **800775** documents match your query.

1. **Yahoo! - U.S. blue chips slash losses, Nasdaq edges higher**
   Yahoo | Write Us | Search | Headlines | Info] [Business - Company - Industry - Finance - PR Newswire - Business Wire - Quotes] Thursday August 14 3:20..
   http://biz.yahoo.com/finance/97/08/14/z0000_21.html - size 4K - 15-Aug-97 - English

2. **SI: BLUE DESERT MINING, BDE-ASE**
   BLUE DESERT MINING, BDE-ASE. Carlson On-line Profile | Started By: Dale Schwartzenhauer Date: Mar 9 1997 12:52AM EST. Investors should check out BDE, one..
   http://www.techstocks.com/~wsapi/investor/Subject-13562 - size 4K - 15-Aug-97 - English

3. **UBL Artist: Daly Planet Blues Band**
   Daly Planet Blues Band. The Daly Planet home page The only resource for info on this jam band from Hilton Head Island, SC. Band info, pictures, contact...
   http://www.ubl.com/artists/009821.html - size 6K - 7-Aug-97 - English

4. **takuroku blues**
   http://www.sainet.or.jp/~akihisa/ - size 242 bytes - 16-Feb-97

5. **From Deep Blue to deep space: Take a panoramic look at Mars' surface**
   Take a panoramic look at Mars' surface. To view the image* below, you'll need to install IBM's PanoramIX plug-in for the Netscape Navigator browser. The...
   http://www.ibm.com/Stories/1997/07/space6.html - size 2K - 30-Jul-97 - English

---

■ Wildcards are useful if you are looking for a word that could be singular or plural (look for dog*, instead of dog to broaden the search results).

■ Other characters that can help limit, filter, and sort results include: %, $, !, | (called the piping symbol), ~ (called the tilde), < (less than), and > (greater than). Check the rules of the individual search engines to see how, or if, these characters can be used.

Major Search Engines and Operators

■ Below is a table of the major search tools and how they use some of the search operators. Be sure to check out the search tips and help sections of the sites that you use frequently to see the most current search options. Search tools are constantly updating and improving their sites in response to users' needs.

Search Tool	Boolean operators	+/–	Grouping Operators	Case Sensitivity
AltaVista	✓	✓	✓	✓
AOL NetFind	✓	✓		
Excite	✓	✓	✓	
HotBot	✓	✓	✓	✓
Infoseek		✓	✓	✓
Lycos		✓	✓	
SavvySearch		✓	✓	
Yahoo	✓	✓	✓	✓

WEB RESOURCES

Use General Sites

◆ America Online ◆ Microsoft Network ◆ Pathfinder

General sites such as America Online and Microsoft Network have become much more than gateways to the World Wide Web. The best of these sites offer rich online content that can eliminate the need to surf and search the sometimes confusing and tangled Web.

At these general sites you can find the day's news, weather, sports, opinion, special interest features, and in some cases travel services, entertainment reviews, and other specialty information. Some sites also offer you the option of tailoring the home page to suit your personal needs.

These sites are bound to improve as they compete for additional subscribers with more and better content. Take advantage of these sites to get a great start to your Web experience every time you log online.

America Online

http://www.aol.com

 The home page for the leading commercial online service provides a well-organized directory of links to dozens of top Web sites along with brief reviews of each site.

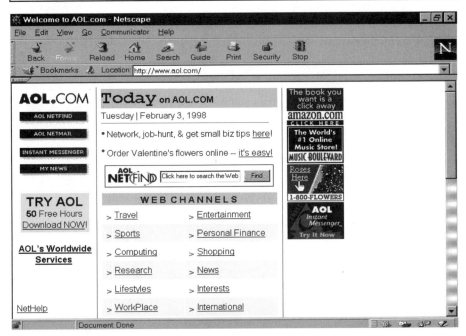

- The AOL Web site isn't just for Internet newcomers and home Web surfers. This site provides a good jumping-off point for any practical Web search.

- The AOL site has a comprehensive and well-organized Web directory, with access to dozens of links to many of the best resources available on the Web. Just click one of the AOL channels to see links to Web sites that AOL has selected as favorites along with a brief descriptive paragraph about each site.

- Though most of the channels are primarily oriented to a consumer audience, you can click the WorkPlace channel to see a very complete directory of business Web site links and associated site reviews.

- A few of the selected favorites on each channel are links to an AOL service available only to AOL members, but you will find many more links to sites available to you on the Web.

- A selection of AOL Web site reviews is arranged at the left side of each channel page. Click one of the review topics to dig down deeper and find more Web site links.

- Another nice feature at the AOL site is the easy access to search engine text boxes, where you can quickly enter a keyword search topic and click to find what you need. Each AOL channel typically showcases two or three Web sites near the top of the channel page by including search engine text boxes for those sites.

- Click the NetFind link to use the very helpful Time Savers directory. Here you will find links to Web resources for many common tasks such as Find an Airline or Hotel, Plan a Night Out, Plan a Night In, Manage Your Investments, Your Health, and Your Government.

- Links to AOL services such as NetMail (Web access e-mail) and Instant Messenger are also featured at the AOL site, but you must be an AOL member to use these services.

Microsoft Network
http://www.msn.com

 This leading computer software developer provides a broad range of online content for technology information, social issues, and entertainment.

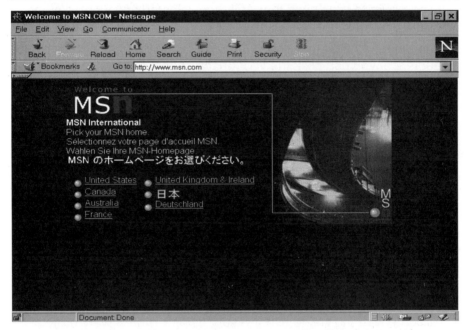

- There has been a pattern over the years when Microsoft enters a promising new market: Microsoft may not offer the first or best product, but after a while, the Microsoft product catches on and then overtakes the competition.

- The same pattern holds true in the commercial online service market. Microsoft Network (MSN) was supposed to take over the world when it was offered as an icon on the Windows 95 desktop several years ago. However, as many people who clicked the icon on their desktop found, the initial content available on MSN usually wasn't worth a second look. In addition, the network connections were typically slow and unreliable.

- Over the past couple of years, MSN's content has vastly improved, even if the network connections remain slow at times. MSN's wide range of consumer and information Web site offerings makes it well worth a stop on your online search.

- Topping the list of MSN sites is the award winning Expedia travel service. Expedia is an example of how much interactivity and rich content can be delivered on a commercial Web site. Expedia's outstanding travel-booking wizard makes it a fine business and sales resource. Sidewalk is a wonderfully complete guide to nine U.S. cities as well as Sydney, Australia.

- Check out Microsoft Investor and Money Insider for a couple of the best investment and market sites available on the Web. Also, try the Computing Central site for computer forums, tips, software downloads, and industry news.

- The Mining Company is a new search site offered by MSN that offers the services of online guides to help you find what you want. Other MSN sites are consumer-oriented, but provide very useful and well-presented resources to help you find out about cars (CarPoint), movies (Cinemania), games (Internet Gaming Zone), music (Music Central), and shopping (Plaza).

Pathfinder

http://pathfinder.com

 Use this easy-to-access directory to find Time Warner media Web sites such as Time, Life, People, Fortune, CNNSI, and Travel & Leisure. Perhaps the most complete and wide-ranging collection of current information available on the Web.

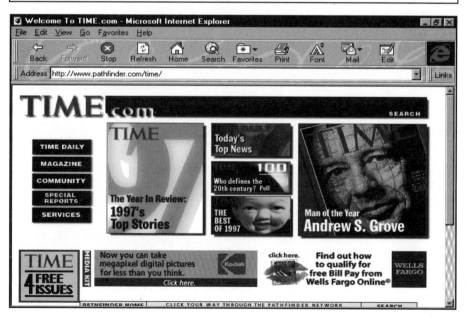

- Time Warner's Pathfinder site brings together all the news, information, and entertainment content of dozens of Web, magazine, and video properties owned by the media conglomerate.

- This site is a great source for news, sports, politics, and entertainment coverage, offering links to Time, CNNSI, People, Entertainment Weekly, Variety Netwire, Life, and AllPolitics.

- The above list is just a sampling of the interesting and informative resources available at Pathfinder. You can also find financial sites such as Fortune, Hoover's Business Resources, Money Daily, Money Online, Portfolio Tracker, and Quick Quotes.

- Get travel news and fares at the Travel & Leisure, WebFlyer, PlanetSurfer, and Magellan Maps sites. Net Culture sites feature PC and Web news and information.

- If you want to shop, click on one of the many Marketplace sites, including BarnesandNoble.com, CDNow, Fortune Book Fair, Internet Shopping Network, and Time Life Photo Sight.

- Pathfinder also provides free e-mail service, a financial calculator, community chat sites, a cyberdating service, and an investment portfolio tracker. This wide-ranging collection of sites may be one of the most comprehensive information sources available on the Web.

Use Directories and Search Engines

◆ **Yahoo!** ◆ **Excite** ◆ **Dogpile** ◆ **Open Text** ◆ **Other Sites**

When you want information on the Web but don't know where to look, the best place to start is a directory or search engine. These sites help organize the vast contents of the Internet and the World Wide Web so that you can focus your search efforts and zoom to the exact Web site (or other Internet service) you need.

Directories Organize the Web

- Though they go about it in different ways, directories and search engines have the same goal—locating information online. Directories provide a map of how information is organized on the World Wide Web. Typically, they break the Web down into a number of categories—usually numbering about a dozen or so.

- Categories might include broad search areas such as arts and humanities, business, computers and Internet, news and media, science, and entertainment. Beyond the main categories, directories typically break Web contents down into finer and finer subcategories. For example, the business category might be split into companies, investing, classifieds, taxes, and more. Searching these layers of subcategories until you find what you need is called "drilling down" in the directory.

Search Engines Comb the Web

- Search engines provide you with readily accessible database search software that searches Web contents or, in some cases, directories or indexes of Web contents. You enter one or more keywords into the search engine's text box, click a button on screen, and then let the software do the work.

- Typically, a search engine will return a listing of results that match your keyword(s) as closely as possible. Many search engines include confidence rankings that indicate how closely the software thinks each result matches your keyword(s). Results may be links to Web sites or links to directory categories or subcategories.

- Search Web sites can include directories, search engines, or both. They may also contain news updates and other content found only at the search site. Each of these sites finds information on the Web differently, and that can help you find what you need faster once you have learned the unique benefits of each site's approach.

Yahoo!

http://www.yahoo.com

Yahoo!, the original Web search site, provides a
well-organized directory of Web contents, a powerful
search engine, and an ever-growing list of new
features that focus on special interests.

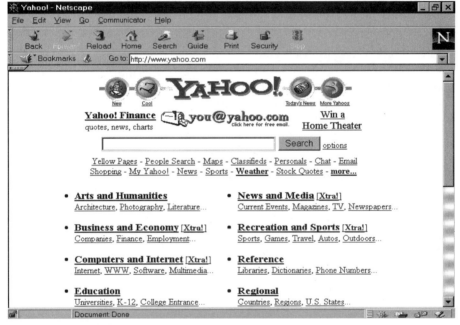

- Perhaps the most recognizable name in the Web searching
  business is Yahoo!, the granddaddy of them all. The site is
  continuously updated and new Yahoo! services are added regularly
  to expand the site. Click on the New icon at the top of the home
  page to see what features have been added recently.

- What Yahoo! does best is organizing the Web. The list of directory
  categories and subcategories on the Yahoo! home page has been
  copied by many other Web search and directory sites. If you have a
  fairly good idea of what you're looking for, click the category (or
  subcategory) link that comes closest to matching your interest.

- After clicking a category link, you will see a page of subcategory
  links. Click one of these to drill down even further in the directory
  structure and narrow your search. After two or three clicks, you
  should start to zero in on links to specific Web sites.

- From the Yahoo! home page you can also click Today's News icon for a quick way to check the day's headlines. Click the More Yahoos icon to see a listing of other Yahoo! services such as My Yahoo! (where you can customize the site to your liking), Get Local (focusing on a Zip Code you specify), Yahoo! Chat (for online talk), and various Yahoo! Metros (focusing on major cities across the country). Click the home page Cool icon to see a directory of more off-the-wall Web site categories.

- You can also search the Yahoo! directories by entering a keyword(s) in the search text boxes available on every page. You can search the entire Yahoo! directory or limit the search to the portion you're currently visiting. Remember, Yahoo! searches only its directories, which consist of Web page titles and descriptions, not the full Web. This yields more focused search results.

Excite

http://www.excite.com

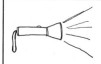

Excite features a tight directory structure and allows searching by concepts, which means you can enter conversational search phrases and get more targeted results.

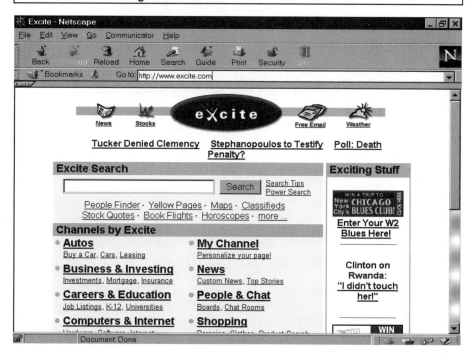

- After trying a few keyword searches, you may come to discover that Web search engines take your keywords very literally. The Excite Web site attempts to solve this problem by enabling you to search by concepts instead of by keywords.

- That is, the Excite search engine knows that words such as "coffee" and "cake" can have different meanings when they are used together from when they are used separately. The Excite engine also knows that words such as "play" can have many meanings, and it takes these into account when you enter a concept phrase.

- The bottom line is that you can use conversational phrases to describe what you want Excite to find. For example, if you're looking for plays by Arthur Miller, just type in "plays by Arthur Miller." If you're looking for sports plays of the day, just type in "sports plays of the day." Excite eliminates the process of deciding what the best keyword strategy will be to get the search results you want.

- Excite also provides a very tight Web directory that includes only three levels of categories. This is a reflection of the more narrow criteria Excite uses to screen sites indexed in its directory.

- You are guaranteed to find links to Web sites by the time you click three Excite category links. You can also read Excite summaries of each site that links to it. The net result for you is a quicker, more informed directory search than you can perform at other directory sites.

- Excite also includes links to features such as News (well-organized directory of wire service reports), Stocks (a business news summary page with stock quotes), TV (a table-style television guide), and Weather (national and local forecasts).

Dogpile

http://www.dogpile.com

 Use this search engine of search engines to look for what you want on 25 Internet search and directory sites.

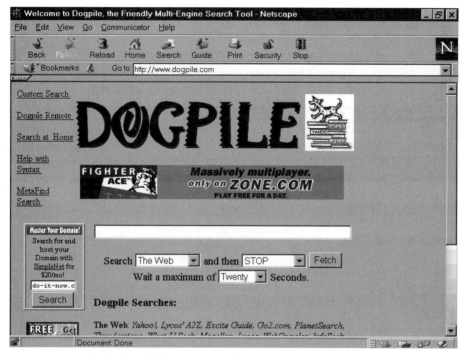

- Want to get the maximum coverage for your search? Try Dogpile. Dogpile is the Internet search site that checks all the other important search and directory sites.

- Enter a keyword search into the Dogpile home page and specify whether you want Dogpile to search the Web, FTP, Usenet, or newswires. You can search a maximum of two of the above and then select a maximum wait time for the search to be completed.

- Click the Fetch button to begin the search. The powerful Dogpile search engine searches 25 different services, including Yahoo!, Excite, Lycos, WebCrawler, InfoSeek, AltaVista, HotBot, DejaNews, and more. You can also specify the order of services in which you want Dogpile to search by clicking on the Custom Search link. You can rest assured that you have thoroughly combed the Internet after finishing a Dogpile search.

- Click on the Help with Syntax link to read a detailed how-to page for using keyword search operators such as AND, OR, NOT, and NEAR. Because some search engines support these keyword operators in different ways, you should check out the Help with Syntax page before constructing any complex Dogpile searches.

Open Text

http://index.opentext.net

 Search every word of the World Wide Web with the Open Text engine.

- When you want to search the entire World Wide Web, use the Open Text search engine. Open Text treats the Web as one gigantic text file. Your keyword search in Open Text is virtually the same as using the Find feature in a word processing document, but in this case the document is the entire Web.

- From the Open Text index page, enter your keyword search in the text box. Click on the search button and wait for a results page to appear.

- Typically, you will get a large number of pages that match your search keyword(s). You can narrow the search by clicking the Power Search link. Then you can enter multiple search keywords, narrow your search to titles, summaries, first headings, or URLs, and use search operators.

- Drop-down list menus in Power Search provide choices for search locations and operators to make selection easier. Remember that the more keywords you use, the narrower your search will be (unless you connect the words with or, which includes all the keywords).

- You can also search current events, e-mail, newsgroups, and other languages. With a little practice and experimentation, Open Text searches can yield pleasantly surprising and highly effective search results.

Other Sites

Infoseek
http://www.infoseek.com

- Search any part of the Web quickly and easily with this widely respected search and directory page. It is easy to perform quick searches as well more complex searches at this site.

Lycos
http://www.lycos.com

- This full-featured search and directory site is famous for its top 5% reviews of Web sites. Its high-powered Custom Search page lets you hone in on the results you need.

DejaNews
http://www.dejanews.com

- This site searches Usenet newsgroups, the Internet's version of online chat bulletin boards. Find experts on a particular topic or just tap into a discussion about a subject of interest.

The Mining Company
http://www.miningcompany.com

- This site takes a unique approach to finding information on the Web, with special interest sections led by "Guides" who specialize in a particular topic area. You can also search the site by interest areas, subsections, or related sites.

Bargains Online

◆ FirstAuction ◆ Planet Shopping Network ◆ eBay Auction Classifieds
◆Other Sites

These days more and more merchants have sites on the Web. With so many merchants, finding bargains on the Net can be daunting. How does the avid shopper cover them all? The answer to one-stop cybershopping is Internet malls, which contain links to dozens of merchants. For bargain hunting on the Web, an Internet auction site may well be the answer. Bid against others for everything from general household merchandise to consumer electronics to vacations.

FirstAuction

http://www.firstauction.com/

 Ever wondered what it would be like to attend an auction? Here's your chance. FirstAuction gives you the chance to bid on a wide variety of products and walk away with some real bargains.

- Joining FirstAuction is easy and may be the start of great bargain hunting on the Net. To become a FirstAuction member you need to submit personal information, decide on a bidder screen name, and enter a major credit card number.

- Once you have registered, you can start bidding on one or more of the many great products featured. You decide how much you want to bid on the products offered, then wait and see what happens. You can increase your bid anytime until the posted auction closing. The auctions are live and the bidding starts periodically throughout the day. Sometimes bidding lasts a couple of days. FlashAuctions, which are offered eleven times a day, last thirty minutes each. Joining FirstAuction is free so you have nothing to loose but a little time. The upside is that you may come away with some real bargains.

- FirstAuction sets the starting bid at a ridiculously low price for a limited quantity of a particular product. All products featured in the FlashAuctions start at $1.00.

- Information about each product offered is available by clicking on the product listing. Click on Starting at (price) for a description of each product.

- FirstAuction Insider will notify you by e-mail if your bid is a winner or if you need to submit a higher bid to stay in the running. They will also notify you by e-mail about upcoming auctions and special promotions. The site features tips on successful bidding and frequently highlights winners in the Winners Spotlight area.

- If you are worried about junk mail as a result of submitting your information to this site, FirstAuction promises that all membership and purchase information is confidential and promises never to provide it to any outside organization for marketing purposes.

Planet Shopping Network

http://www.planetshopping.com/

So you like the mall but your schedule only allows the occasional visit. Planet Shopping Network lets you shop the mall from the comfort of your computer.

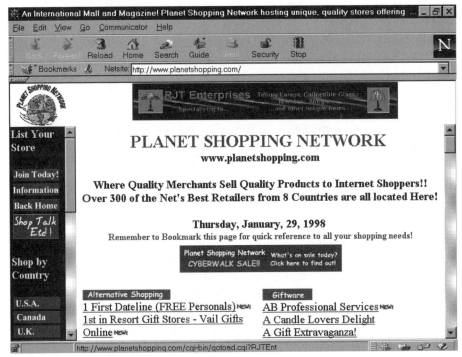

- The Planet Shopping Network has over 300 merchants from 8 countries. American merchants include Wal-Mart, LL Bean, Legg's, Omaha Steaks, and JC Penny. There are also lesser known merchants like the Pet Warehouse Catalog and the Bridalink Store.

- Cybershopping is easy. Just click on the link to the store of your choice and then click the link to the desired department. You will see what each store offers online and you can purchase any of the goods offered using a major credit card via a secure server located at the store site.

- In many cases there are online specials that you wouldn't find if you went directly to the store. On the other hand, many sites don't offer their entire inventory online. The trade-off, however, is minimal.

- Click on Shop Talk Etc!!, to find out what other shoppers have to say about stores on the network, fashion ideas, as well as links to Grooming Tips, Horoscopes, Music Reviews, and Sporting Life.

- With only a couple of exceptions, such as the Italy site, product descriptions on the foreign country pages are in English, but pricing is displayed in the currency of the country. You can shop any of the stores on the International sites using a major credit card. Several of the foreign sites provide an exchange rate area so that you can calculate the cost in US dollars. Otherwise you will need to know international currency exchange rates.

eBay Auction Classifieds

http://cayman.ebay.com/aw/index.html

If you love second-hand stores, antique shops, or memorabilia, this is the site for you. Browse through the eBay Auction Classifieds and bid on the item of your choice or list items you want to sell with eBay Auction Classifieds.

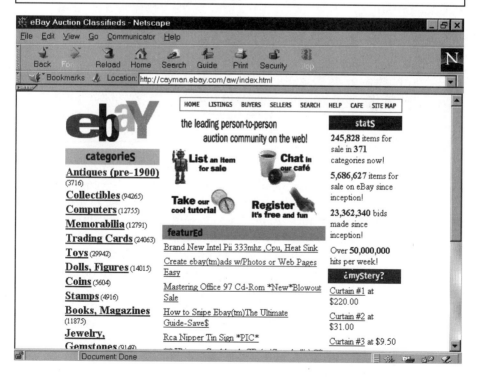

- eBay is the longest running, person-to-person auction house on the Net. You can think of it as a cyber trading post. Items are arranged in 300 separate categories and subcategories. For that hard-to-find item, this may be the site for you.

- The first thing you must do before you bid or sell is register with eBay. This involves providing your e-mail address as well as your real name, address, and contact phone number. You will also need to fill out category interest information. This information is necessary for eBay to put registered buyers and sellers in touch with each other. They promise never to use this information for marketing, nor will they disclose this information to any outside party.

- If you have something to sell, you can list it with eBay in their auction classifieds the same way you would your local newspaper classifieds. What makes this site different from most auction houses on the Net is that eBay sells items person-to-person and not through the manufacturer via the site. Almost all communication between buyer, seller, and eBay is done through e-mail. Check the site for more information about communication procedures.

- Click on any of the category links and begin searching for that special item. Once you have found it, you can bid. If your bid is a winner, the only cost to you is the bid amount, which you pay directly to the seller.

- Bidding is easy, as eBay bids on your behalf. You tell them the maximum amount you are willing to bid, and they will continue to bid as necessary until someone outbids your maximum amount. Your maximum amount is kept confidential and, with luck, may never be reached.

- Selling is also easy, although a bit more involved. First of all, to sell an item on the eBay site, you must pay a series of nominal fees. All fees are based on the value of the item. For example, at the time this book was published, an item worth over $50.00 would be charged a listing fee of $2.00 and 2.5% of the final sale amount. Go to the site for a full list of fees and conditions.

- If you have questions as you navigate the site, eBay offers excellent step-by-step Help features.

Other Sites

CyberShop

http://cybershop.com/

- CyberShop is the world's first online department store open 24 hours a day, 7 days a week, 365 days a year. CyberShop has over 40,000 brand-name products from more than 400 manufacturers.

SaveMeTheMoney.com

http://savemethemoney.com/

- New products arrive on a daily basis at this cyberstore. Links to goods range from stereo equipment, jewelry, computers, and gift items. A full description for each item is available by clicking on the item link.

NETIS

http://www.netis.com/auctions/

- The NETIS site has the most comprehensive listing of worldwide auction information on the Web. For information on real estate, antiques, collector cars, and auctions, to name a few, this is your site. Search for auction information by city, state, or county.

Gourmet Goodies Online

◆ **Virtual Vineyards** ◆ **Fancy Foods Gourmet Club** ◆ **Other Sites**

If you feel life's many pleasures can be summed up by the words "food and drink," then you'll be in for some tasty treats at these great gourmet sites. The offerings in this section will please the most discriminating palates. If you love to cook or want a prepared feast delivered to your door, these sites will show you how to get gourmet goodies online.

Virtual Vineyards

http://www.virtualvin.com/

Wine is the operative word at this site. Choose from hundreds of wines from many small but important vineyards in a wide range of categories and prices.

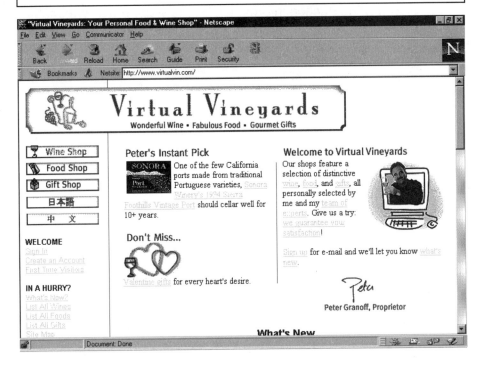

- For the wine connoisseur or the wine novice, Virtual Vineyards has something for everyone. They offer delicious wines from small vineyards. The site provides a comprehensive description of each featured vineyard and detailed information about the wines they offer. In every case, you have a real sense of what you're buying.

- Virtual Vineyards frequently offers specials on selected wines. Go to the Bang for the Buck and the Under 15 dollars for wine specials. Discounted wines tend to move quickly and the selections change frequently, so check the site often.

- If you are serious about wanting to try new wines on a regular basis, enroll in the Virtual Vineyards Monthly Wine Program. You decide how many bottles you would like to receive each month and whether you want all red, all white, or a mixed selection. Most wines have a retail value of $15-$17 as a maximum price. Wine prices vary depending on the monthly selections, but the cost will never exceed the maximum range.

- Search the wine list database by category, grape varietal, or by vineyard.

- Click the Cookware link to find an assortment of corkscrews, stoppers, wine racks, and much more. The Virtual Vineyards Cellar & Kitchen Library (click on Cookbooks) lists books on wine and food recipes.

- If you would like to give wine as a gift but have no idea what to buy, choose a gift certificate. Gift certificates range from $25-$500 and are sent with a gift card and instructions on how to use the certificate to order wines from Virtual Vineyards. Creative gifts of food and wine are available from the online gift shop.

- You need a major credit card to set up an account. Most items are shipped within two days of receipt of the order. Check the site for shipping options.

Fancy Foods Gourmet Club
http://www.ffgc.com/

This site is not for the casual cook. The information contained is dedicated to visitors who have a certain dedication to the art of cooking and fine food.

- The Fancy Foods Gourmet Club online catalog is filled with pages of fine foods for the discriminating palate. The Fancy Foods catalog is distinguished not only by numerous awards for their food products, but also by their quality, limited availability, and great prices.

- All items are 20-50% below average gourmet shop prices. Shop this site for the best in caviar, cheeses, chocolates, pâtés, and desserts. However, don't get too carried away: expensive shipping fees for perishable food can really add up.

- Links to catalog pages are listed by category type. Each page has a limited assortment of elegant products. You can purchase items simply by typing the quantity next to the item listing and clicking the Add to Cart button at the bottom of the screen. You then have the option to continue shopping or proceed to the checkout.

- You can also purchase such delicacies as olives, roasted garlic, and basil oils in decorative bottles. In addition, Fancy Foods has caviar dishes and spoons, a full kit of Indian spices, an assortment of truffles, and vinegars. Definitely upscale. Wonderfully decadent.

- From the Gift Sets page you can select from a variety of baskets, such as the CHOCOLATE LOVERS basket, which contains nine assorted truffles, chocolate chambord sauce, and omenene ingots made from Ghanian cocoa beans. As of January 1998, this basket was selling for $55. Basket selections include SOME LIKE IT HOT, which contains hot sauces, mustards, and salsa, and for the seafood fan you can purchase THE U.S. STURGEON GENERAL'S BOX.

- Fuli gourmet meals are also available for purchase. The menus range from scones and gourmet jellies for breakfast in bed to hearty seafood dinner extravaganzas that include smoked Coho salmon, duck liver mousse, and raspberry linzer tortes.

- The quality of all the items offered by the Fancy Foods Gourmet Club is guaranteed. You can order online with a Visa or MasterCard.

Other Sites

Epicurious

http://www.epicurious.com/

- This site is for the passionate cook. It contains over 7,500 recipes from Gourmet and Bon Appetit magazines. Epicurious also includes wine suggestions, restaurants of note, and useful cooking tips.

The Brewery—Total Homebrewing Info

http://realbeer.com/brewery/

- Everything you want to know about home brewing beer can be found on this site. They have an extensive library and links with relevant information on brewing techniques and products.

Wine Navigator

http://homearts.com/helpers/winenav/wine.htm

- The Wine Navigator can help you choose the right wine for the right price. There are links to a glossary of terms, tips on buying and storing wine, and advice on how to match wine with food.

Ridiculously Easy Recipes for Students and Other Incompetents

http://sar.usf.edu/~zazuetaa/recipe.html

- Auntie Boo is the keeper of this site. Each of the recipes listed has been tried by Ms. Boo and comes with a foolproof guarantee. Proceed with caution.

Plan and Book Travel Online

◆ **Microsoft Expedia** ◆ **Bed and Breakfast Inns Online** ◆ **Zagat Survey**
◆ **MapQuest** ◆ **Other Sites**

Use the Web to make your next vacation more enjoyable and more cost effective. There are dozens of excellent travel-related sites that can help you plan your trip, search for bargains, and book tickets online. These top travel Web sites provide a good sample of the kinds of resources available online to help you.

Microsoft Expedia

http://expedia.msn.com/daily/home/default.hts

Use this award-winning Web site to explore destinations, plan your trip itinerary, and book travel online.

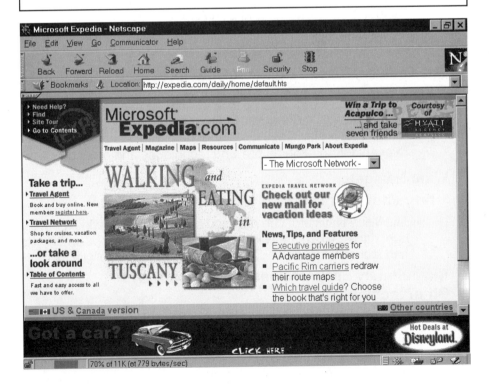

- Microsoft Expedia is the award-winning travel Web site produced by the software giant as part of its Microsoft Network online service. The site has been named one of the top 100 Web sites by PC Magazine, a Yahoo! Internet Life Five-Star Award winner (one of only twelve per year), and a Top Ten PCWeek E-Commerce winner.

- The site receives these awards with good reason. First, its Web page design is a pleasure to view. Second, it's chock-full of information about where to go and what to do. Click on the Resources link to browse the World Guide, a complete online travel guidebook, check weather, and use a currency converter.

- Click on Magazine to read articles about travel destinations, news briefs, bargain updates, as well as featured columnists and ideas about fresh approaches to travel that can make your trip more enjoyable.

- The beauty of most travel Web sites is the capability to plan and book travel online. Expedia offers a number of powerful search and booking tools at its Travel Agent link. You can also search for available hotel rooms at your destination and reserve rooms. If you need a rental car, you can find and reserve one here, too.

Bed and Breakfast Inns Online

http://www.bbonline.com

 Bed and Breakfast Inns are a distinctive alternative to hotels and motels. Distinctive, however, does not have to mean expensive. Let Bed and Breakfast Inns Online show you how.

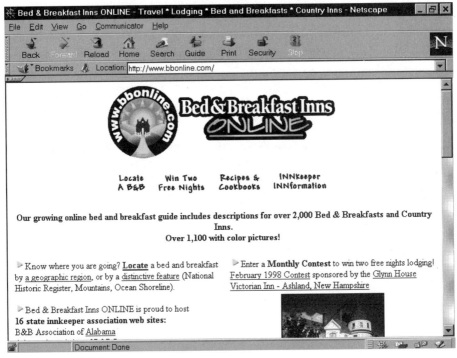

- It's all a matter of taste, but one way to make travel more enjoyable is to avoid cookie-cutter chain hotels and stay at a small inn that lets you experience a little more of what life is like in the town you're visiting.

- Bed & Breakfast Inns Online provides a guide to more than 2,000 bed and breakfasts and country inns across the United States. You may be surprised by how many fine inns are available at very reasonable rates, in many cases less expensive than staying at a chain hotel.

- Many inns and bed and breakfasts are located in major cities, close to the center of town. Click on the Locate a B&B link at the Bed & Breakfast Inns Online home page to begin your search.

- You can search the site's database by location in the United States, Canada, Mexico, and the Caribbean. U.S. listings are organized by region and then by state.

- You can also search for inns by distinctive features, such as being by the ocean or in the mountains, being on the National Register of Historic Places, having special accommodations for horses, or those offering special package deals. The site also includes links to state innkeeper association Web sites.

Zagat Survey

http://www.pathfinder.com/travel/Zagat

 Find the right restaurant for your next night out by consulting the Zagat Survey online. This site offers a complete directory of survey listings and reviews for 40 major U.S. cities.

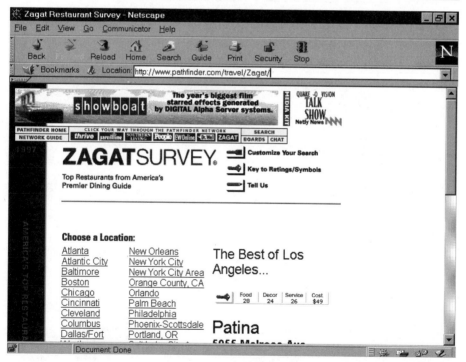

- What could be worse than dropping big bucks on a meal for a night out on the town and having the fare turn out to be downright awful? Consulting the Zagat Survey Web site beforehand is a great way to avoid ruining what could turn out to be a perfectly delicious evening.

- The Zagat Survey is widely recognized as the leading guide to fine dining across the country. Click on a city link to view an alphabetical index of restaurant listings for the city. You can also search the listing directory by cuisine, by food ranking, or by best deals.

- If you already know the name of the restaurant you want to find, just type it into the search engine text box and click Find It!

- Each link to a restaurant has a brief description of the type of cuisine (such as French, vegetarian, or Tex-Mex) to help you sift among the many possibilities. Click on a restaurant link to read the Zagat review. The survey rates each restaurant by food, decor, and service on a scale of 0 to 30. The cost of an average dinner plus drink and tip is also listed.

MapQuest

http://www.mapquest.com

 You never have to worry about getting lost again. Check the MapQuest site for door-to-door driving directions and interactive maps of any location in the continental U.S.

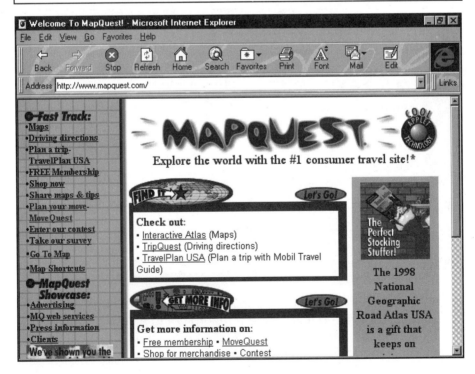

- Click on the TripQuest link for driving directions from your starting point to your destination.

- You can choose from several mapping options, including city-to-city, door-to-door for 29 major metro areas, turn-by-turn maps with text, or text only. City-to-city routing is provided for any town or city within the continental U.S. and some parts of Mexico and Canada.

- To find your own way, click on the Interactive Atlas link on the home page. From there, you can enter a point of interest or an address to view a map of that location. A zoom feature allows you to view more or less area of detail on the maps.

- Click on the TravelPlan USA link at the MapQuest home page to plan your next trip using the Mobil Travel Guide.

Other Sites

The Trip

http://www.thetrip.com

- Among the many travel Web sites available, The Trip stands out because of its attention to the needs of road travelers. The Trip has a no-nonsense, no-hassle approach to planning and booking enjoyable travel.

Subway Navigator

http://metro.jussieu.fr:10001/bin/cities/english

- Find subway or rail system routes in major cities around the world.

Travlang Foreign Languages for Travelers

http://www.travlang.com

- This extensive directory of language resources for study and translation includes links to sites for even the most obscure languages. The site also offers international hotel listings, air reservations, and currency exchange information.

Cheap Seats (Airfare)

◆ FareBusters ◆ 1Travel.com ◆ Other Sites

If you're looking for the cheapest airfares available, try online discount travel sites. The cheap seats are generally for travel on major airline carriers and often the prices are lower than advertised sale fares. As an added bonus, you can often make hotel and car rental arrangements at these sites.

FareBusters

http://www.farebusters.com/

So you're looking for cheap seats. Well you've come to the right place. FareBusters has cheap airfares and lots of them. If you don't believe that this site has the cheapest fares around, click on the Comparison link from their home page and see for yourself.

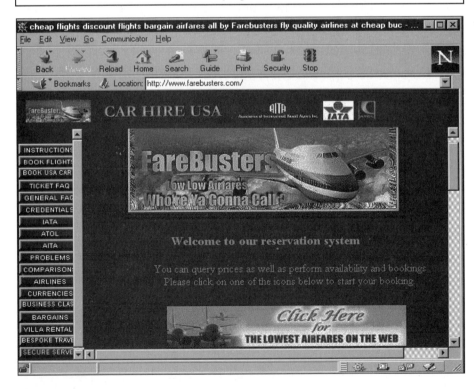

136

- The first thing you should know about this site is that FareBusters is a European outfit. This will explain why you may find yourself on a page written in German or why the word "Class" is spelled "Klasse" when inputting fare requests.

- You can access the fare database by clicking Enter. Or, click the "FareBusters Who You Gonna Call?" graphic link at the top of the home page, click the American flag icon, and follow the on screen instructions. Because the server is on a site somewhere in Europe and the site is very popular, user traffic may conspire against you. A little patience may be required but the fares are well worth any inconvenience you may experience.

- Once you click the Enter button on the home page, query the FareBusters database by typing in your departure and the destination city, selecting your trip dates from the drop-down menus, the class of service you desire, and the number of passengers traveling. Then click the Query Fares button. Your query will return several fare and airline carrier options.

- To see how the FareBusters' costs compare to those being offered by other agencies, click the Comparison button from the static side bar on the site.

- You can book and pay for your tickets online via the FareBusters secure server or book the ticket and, within 48 hours, an agent will contact you to arrange payment. To get further information on ticketing, click the Ticket FAQ link on the left-hand side of any page.

- If you are a little uneasy about booking discount airline tickets with an agency so far from home, click on IATA on the side bar. This page outlines FareBusters' credentials and describes in detail the many ways in which your interests are protected. You can also click on the General FAQ link for more information.

- FareBusters offers discounts on accommodations and hotel alternatives (Villas) as well as providing details on car rentals in your destination city. For the international traveler, go to the Currency page for conversion rates.

1travel.com

http://1travel.com/Welcome.htm

 You can find cheap domestic and international airfares for travel on almost every major airline carrier. Use their interactive database of fares and flight information to find bargains. You can also check airline regulations and your rights as a passenger.

- 1travel.com is a ticket consolidator. Ticket consolidators buy tickets in bulk to hundreds of destinations from many different airlines. The great thing about 1travel.com is that they cut out the middle people (i.e., travel agents) and offer deeply discounted fares directly to the public.

- Unlike many discount fare sites that only offer discounted round-trip fares, you can find discounts on one-way fares, business class, and first class fares to select destinations.

- Check out Last Minute Deals for weekly specials offered on fifteen different carriers. You can register to receive 1travel.com special offers and last minute airfare discounts by clicking the Sign-Up For Email ALERT!s link on the Last Minute Deals page. Information will be automatically sent to you weekly.

- Click the Travel Guide link on the home page for general information on your destination (city or country) including weather, vital statistics, and tourism contacts. The Travel Guide gives more extensive information for international destinations, including a history of many countries, the exchange rates, health services, accommodations, and holidays and events.

- 1travel.com also has a unique link called Rules of the Air. This link answers questions you may have concerning check-in times and carry-on baggage limits by airline. It also outlines your rights as a passenger, if, for example, your flight is overbooked or what your options are if your flight is delayed.

- Click the Currency Exchange link found at the bottom of the home page to purchase foreign currencies by mail from International Currency Express, Inc. 1travel.com claims to have the best exchange rates anywhere—even better than American Express or Thomas Cook. You may order currencies by telephone or online order form with a credit card, check, or money order.

- You can also get information on renting apartments or villas as an alternative to hotels.

Other Sites

The Air Traveler's Handbook

http://www.cs.cmu.edu/afs/cs.cmu.edu/user/mkant/ Public/Travel/airfare.html

- This comprehensive site links you to resources on airline ticket consolidators and "bucket shops," FAQs on frequent flyer programs, Online Computer Reservations Systems, and where to get tourist and travel information.

Casto Travel, Inc.

http://www.casto.com/resource/travel_insurance.cfm

- There are links to travel insurance for the casual and business traveler. Search the Travel Resource Index for information on everything from ski reports to kids' travel tips to discount airfares. There are also great links for the physically challenged traveler.

Lonely Planet Online

http://www.lonelyplanet.com/

- Lonely Planet Online is a bit irreverent, but they discuss almost anything you want to know about traveling on your own. They provide maps, travel information, photos, and historical and cultural information about every continent on the planet. Hip and very informative.

FareFinder

http://www.reservations.com/Farefinder/

- To find the lowest airfares available, check Preview Travel's FareFinder service. Enter your departure and destination cities to find the lowest fares currently available.

Personal Finance

◆ ValueLine ◆ Wall Street Research Net ◆ Other Sites

There was a time when putting away a nest egg was limited to a low interest-bearing savings account or a company retirement plan. Now, more people are preparing for their financial futures by taking action and investing their money. Information on how to play the financial field is more accessible than ever, thanks, in part, to resources on the Internet.

ValueLine

http://www.valueline.com/

ValueLine can not only help you understand the world of investing, but can also help you assess your financial goals and build the investment portfolio you desire.

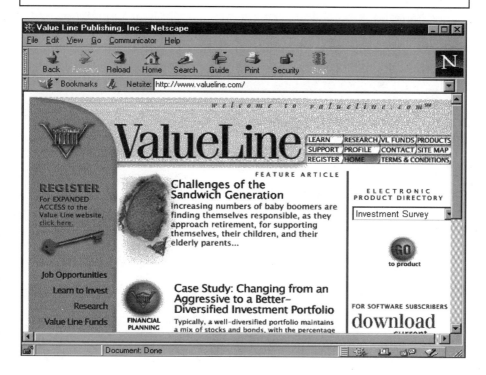

- ValueLine is an all-purpose investment organization. In order to gain expanded access to this site, you must first fill out a short online registration form. Although you can view many of the areas on this site without registering, your registration ID and password will give you full run of the site.

- The Glossary of Investment Terms, on the Learn to Invest page, makes it easy for you to get up to speed on basic investment lingo and actually helps you acquire general knowledge about how to invest. The definitions are brief and easy to understand. Some terms, such as Common Stock and Mutual Funds, have links to more thorough definitions.

- You can read featured articles on financial planning, mutual funds, and stocks from past ValueLine publications by clicking the Research link from the ValueLine table of contents at the top of the page.

- There are numerous investment portfolios on the ValueLine Funds page from an Aggressive Income Trust to a U.S. Government Securities Fund. Click the ValueLine Funds link for more information on the investment portfolios available.

- A wide range of investing information is available in ValueLine publications. ValueLine Products and Services lists links to many electronic and print publications for your consideration. There are also links to institutional services. Each product is listed with a telephone number or service description for more information. In addition, technical support is available for all electronic publications.

- If you've always dreamed of a job in the field of investing, the Help Wanted area lists job opportunities available at ValueLine.

Wall Street Research Net
http://www.wsrn.com/

Wall Street Research Net has over 500,000 links in their research database. You can watch stock markets around the world and access investor information to make informed decisions when it comes to your personal finances.

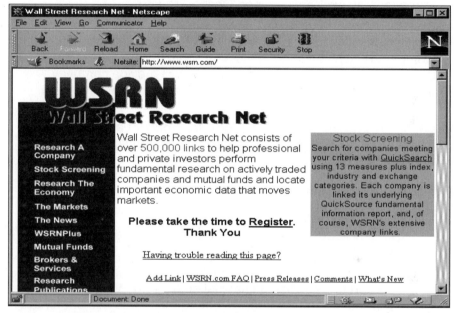

- The Wall Street Research Net site's focus is on providing information to investors. With eight major categories (company information, market news, general news, research publications, mutual funds, brokers and services, and new Web resources) and over 500,000 links, this site is essential for both professional and private investors.

- When you begin to use this site, WSNR encourages you to register with them. Registration is basically a user poll, but once you're registered you can choose to be informed when WSNR updates or adds to the site.

- The largest of these sections is the Company Information section. Click Research A Company to go there. From this page you can access 17,000 company listings and over 2,000 company home page links. You can find a company by ticker symbol from the alphabetical listing or by full or partial name. Most listings have links to information like SEC documents, annual reports, press releases and other investor information, stock quotes, graphs, audio, and more.

- Access Market Summaries from the Dow Jones Industrial, New York Stock Exchange, American Stock Exchange, and the NASDAQ Stock Exchange from The Markets page. These pages cover the current day's earnings, earnings surprises, earnings estimates, and announcements.

- Click on Brokers & Services to get personalized financial and investment information, through over 100 links to brokerage firms and financial services agencies. There are also links to Investment Managers, News Services, and Online Trading.

- WSRN CompanyWatch is a convenient way to keep track of the companies in your portfolio. From the home page, click About WSRN CompanyWatch to find out about this service. After you complete an online registration form, CompanyWatch will provide company information, press releases, and charts for each U.S. traded company in your portfolio.

- Based on your input, such as price, yield, growth and size criteria, and ratios, use WSRN QuickSearch to find companies that fit your specifications.

Other Sites

OSU Virtual Finance Library

http://www.cob.ohio-state.edu/dept/fin/cern/cerninv.htm

- This Web site is maintained by the Ohio State University Department of Finance and probably has the most comprehensive list of financial sites on the Web. OSU has won numerous awards, validating their status as one of the best financial resources on the Net.

CyberPACE Online Bill Payment

http://www.pacecu.org/onlineserv/online_bill_payment.html

- For a small fee this company will arrange for you to pay your bills online. For each bill, you decide how much you want to pay and when you want to pay it and CyberPACE does the rest. Just complete the CyberPACE authorization form, and once you receive your welcome kit and instructions, turn on your computer to start paying bills.

National Association of Investors Corporation

http://www.better-investing.org/

- NAIC is dedicated to investment education. As a member and investor, you are eligible to receive products, services, and professional support. You can join as an individual member, or start an investment club and join as a group.

Movie Lovers' Online Resources

◆ Reel ◆ International Movie Database ◆ Moviefinder.com ◆ Other Sites

One of the great things about the Internet is that you don't have to leave the comfort of your computer to access many of life's simple pleasures. This section is for movie lovers and contains the ultimate movie rental, purchase, and general cinema resource Web sites.

Reel

http://www.reel.com/

Reel is *the* one-stop video movie rental and purchase site. Search their database for information on thousands of video titles.

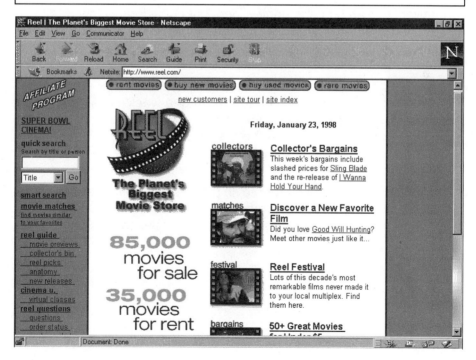

- Reel boasts that they are the biggest movie store on the planet. They claim to have over 50,000 movies for sale and over 35,000 movies for rental. For hard to find domestic and foreign titles, this is the place to go. Search the Reel database by title, actor, or director. Reel also provides video recommendations by genre.

- Before you can rent or purchase a movie, you must first set up an account using a major credit card, and you must be at least 18 years old.

- If you do not have a major credit card or would rather order videos by check, money order, or purchase order, you can submit the order and Reel will e-mail the cost to you. Contact the site for more information.

- Movies are offered in many different formats. Among the formats offered are VHS, DVD, laser, and letterbox, although not all titles are available in all formats.

- The rental policy: keep the movies for one week and return them in the box in which they came. The rental is $4.50 per movie plus postage ($3.50 per video plus postage if you rent 5 titles or more). At the time this book was published, the standard shipping and handling was $6.50 for a single video, but considerably lower for multiple video rentals. Shipping and handling costs include the return postage. You can have your order shipped faster than the standard (3-10 days) delivery time but it will cost more.

- The videos arrive accompanied by a preaddressed label and a metered postage stamp for the return. After a week's time, put the films back in the box, seal it with the tape strips provided, attach the postage stamp, and drop it in the mailbox. There is a $.65 per day late fee charged on films kept more than a week. The late charge stops accruing on the date of the return postmark.

- Reel also has great prices for movie purchases. With over 50,000 titles for sale, there is a wide range of prices depending on the title and format. You can also choose from many titles in the $5-$10 range.

International Movie Database
http://www.imdb.com/

This site is a movie lover's dream. There is more information than you will ever need to know on what appears to be every movie ever made. With weekly columns and a user-friendly database of facts and figures, this is one of the Web's best movie resources.

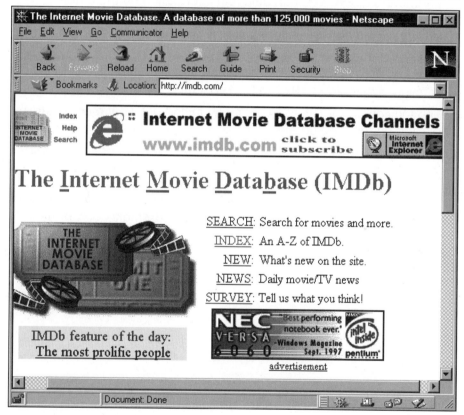

- The Internet Movie Database has information on over 120,000 movies and over 1,750,000 filmography entries. Click the gold movie ticket and begin your search.
- The database gives movie plot summaries, character names, movie ratings, running times, and the entire film personnel from actors to directors to technicians.

- The hardcore cinephile can find information on effects companies, sound mixes, filming locations, movie trivia, and filming goofs. Not to mention official studio pages, technical data, and direct links for movie and memorabilia purchases and rentals.

- It is very easy to navigate this extensive database because of the numerous search options. You can search by title, cast or crew members, year, genre, or country.

- IMDb includes feature sections such as the Washed-UPdate, a gossip column about your favorite actors and movie productions around the globe. You can also find information on the births, deaths, and marriages of movie folks on any given day in history by clicking on the Movie History link and clicking on the desired date.

- Click on the Academy Awards link to find everything you could possibly want to know about Academy Award-nominated and winning movies from 1927 to the present.

- The Movies on TV link is a quick way to find out what movies are playing on the tube on any given day.

- The Internet Movie Database is supported by sponsors of the site. When you see a "Buy" button anywhere on the site it indicates a link to one of the IMDb sponsors for the purchase or rental of the video displayed. IMDb asks that you contact the sponsor sites directly and let them know of any transaction that was extremely good or bad.

Moviefinder.com

http://www.moviefinder.com/

If you want to rent a movie or go to the movies, read a movie review or watch a good movie on TV, this site is fun and informative and a definite for movie lovers.

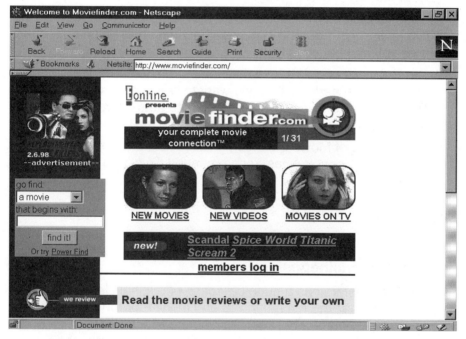

- Let's say you want to go to the movies on Friday night, but you don't know what you want to see. Click on the link to NEW MOVIES for details on current flicks. For each new release there is a fact sheet listing the cast, crew, movie studio, and, for many of the films, a video clip from the film that you can download. Each listing on the sheet contains a filmography link for more information on an actor, crewmember, or studio.

- Once you have decided which movie you want to see, select the when/where link at the top of the movie fact sheet screen or "where" from the currently playing movie list to find out where the movie is playing in your area. The only way to guarantee that you can get a ticket to a popular film is to arrive really early or, if you don't mind sending credit card information over the Internet, order the tickets online. Follow on screen instructions to order tickets online.

- If you want to know what other film buffs have to say about a particular film, click on the Reader Reviews link. You can also submit your own review by clicking on the Grade Movies link but first you must register to become a member of E! Online. Membership is free.

- Click on NEW VIDEOS for video cast and crew facts (complete with filmography links), reviews, and links to outside vendors from whom you can rent or buy the video.

- Select MOVIES ON TV to check TV movie highlights, including pay-per-view listings. Again, you have to become an E! Online member before you can get specific information on listings in your area.

- As an E! Online member, use the Remind Me feature to be reminded when a movie that you want to see is coming to a theater near you. The Remind Me service can also be used to prompt you when a movie is available on video or will be on TV.

- Other features of Moviefinder.com include lists and links for the all-time worst and best movies, recommended films, and links to other cinema hot spots.

Other Sites

Cineposters

http://www.cineposters.com/

- Cineposters has a huge collection of original film posters dating back to the early '70s and many reproductions of classic and recent films. Click on the Movie Posters link and search for posters by actor, director, movie genre, or title.

Ain't It Cool

http://www.aint-it-cool-news.com/

- This is the super hip, ultra cool, no-nonsense movie resource. Ain't It Cool is casual and contains movie information you may never find anywhere else. Don't let the casual tone fool you—this is serious stuff. It's also great fun.

Couch Potato Resources

◆ Gist TV Listings ◆ The UltimateTV Home Page ◆ Other Sites

As art reflects life, TV reflects our culture and times. Your viewing preferences may be highbrow, lowbrow, or a bit of both—there's something for everyone on the tube. The best TV sites on the Web help you out if you're having a hard time finding the right programs.

Gist TV Listings

http://www.thegist.com/

 Imagine having a TV listing tailored to your taste and specifications, a listing with only the TV shows you like, broadcast during the times you watch TV. It's as easy as becoming a member of the GIST TV family.

- GIST has listings for over 11,000 cable and satellite services, as well as time zone lineups. You don't have to become a GIST member to search the TV listings database but it sure makes life a lot easier. The great thing about becoming a member is that you can tailor the TV listing information based on your preferences and avoid wading through hundreds of unwanted TV listings.

- Once you become a member, go to the Preferences area to select the network and cable channels you want included in your personalized listing.

- In addition to choosing channel preferences, choose your favorite times to watch TV, categories of TV programming, and your preferred way to display information.

- Search the database by actor, show title, or multiple words. You can also do a search based only on the criteria you entered in the preferences area during your registration. Once the search results are displayed, each listing is linked to additional information.

- Choose from eight different categories such as Drama, Sci-Fi, Sports, Comedy, Docu/News, or Kids programming.

The UltimateTV Home Page

http://www.ultimatetv.com/news/

UltimateTV keeps you abreast of new TV shows, plots and cast lists, and merchandising that reflects our TV culture. This site is a must-see for TV enthusiasts.

- According to this site, The UltimateTV Show List contains 9,721 links for 1,280 shows, including 1,320 Web pages. If these figures are correct, there is not a more comprehensive site about television on the Web.

- Search the UltimateTV Show List for new mid-season shows added to the TV lineup or browse TV shows by title in the alphabetical listings. You can also search by category like action, miniseries, soap operas, and public access programming.

- The UltimateTV Show List also lets you browse by TV resources for links to Web pages, episode guides, and e-mail addresses for your favorite show's Web site. Instructions for linking directly to your favorite show and questions about The UltimateTV Show List can be found on the Help section and can be accessed from the home page.

- To gain full access to this site, you must join the UltimateTV family by filling out the online form. When you fill out the form, you automatically get a chance to win a classic TV T-shirt and discounts from the TV Store.
- At the TV Store you can buy "I Love Lucy" and "Drew Carey Show" mugs, or "Babylon 5" and "Andy Griffith Show" T-shirts. All merchandise can be purchased online with Visa, MasterCard, or money order.
- You can go to the chat area to talk online to other TV fans, get transcripts of online chats with TV stars, submit your review of a new show, or locate fans of your favorite old show.

Other Sites

Student.com
http://www.student.com/tv/

- Type in the name of the TV show you are looking for and Student.com will display the times, dates, channels and subjects of the show. The site's search engine allows you to search using fairly complex criteria. This site is geared for students but is great for anyone. They will remind you by e-mail of a favorite show, episode or movie.

TV Now Entertainment
http://www.tv-now.com/index.html

- Here you will find a TV Viewer Forum with answers to viewer questions and inside scoops in entertainment. Click the stars on TV link to search through a database of over 700 star appearances each month to find out when your favorite star will be on TV. There are also video appearance listings and links to star Web sites.

The Museum of Television and Radio
http://www.mtr.org/

- Almost any program that has ever been seen on TV can be found at the Museum of Television and Radio. The site includes general information on the advent of television and radio.

Total TV
http://www.tottv.com/

- Total TV is not just another TV guide listing. Total TV allows you to search for a TV show or movie by time, day, program, or movie title or category.

Web Culture

◆ **Louvre Museum** ◆ **Culturefinder** ◆ **Other Sites**

For research or enjoyment, you can experience the finest culture the world has to offer from the comfort of your computer.

Louvre Museum

http://www.culture.fr/louvre/

The Louvre Museum, originally designed as a palace, has been open for over two centuries. It's the biggest and, for works by the great masters, the greatest collection of art in the world.

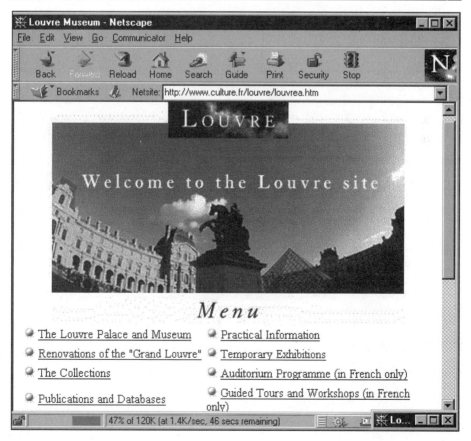

- Even the most casual art lover will be amazed by the exhibits at the Louvre Museum site. There are links to some of the most stunning collections of art on the Web. Unless you read French fluently, the first thing you will need to do is click on the English link at the bottom of the home page.

- Click on The Collections link from the home page and follow links to Oriental, Egyptian, Greek, Etruscan, and Roman antiquities, as well as paintings, sculptures, objets d'art, prints, and drawings from the modern age.

- The Practical Information link displays hours of operation and visitor information while the Temporary Exhibitions link offers information on exhibitions that will be or are currently on display but not part of the permanent collection.

Culturefinder

http://www.culturefinder.com/index.htm

 If you are intimidated by the idea of exploring the Arts but want to get your feet wet, or want a basic guide to cultural news and events, come to Culturefinder.

- One of the most refreshing things about this site is the casual air with which seemingly highbrow topics are presented. Here you will find everything from dance techniques to local classical music radio stations to the top 10 CDs you need to begin your jazz collection.

- To learn more about classical music, opera, dance, or just the arts in general, go to the Ask the Answer Wizards page. Submit questions to the Answer Wizards for short and informative answers to topics on classical music, dance, opera, musical theater, or piano. You can also read questions submitted by others and the Wizard's answers.

- Culturefinder sponsors Celebrity Artist Chats online. Artist Chats, hosted by a Culturefinder representative, gives AOL members a chance to ask artists like Bobby McFerrin, Andre Watts, and Samuel Ramey about their craft, great career moments, and big career mistakes. You can join these chats on AOL or read the transcripts in the Artists Chats area.

- If theater is your thing, click the Broadway 101 link to find out what's playing on and off-Broadway. Read reviews, purchase discount tickets, locate art shops, and find Broadway area restaurants.

- To get a full listing of season schedules for over 1100 arts organizations in the U.S. and Canada, go to The Calendar. You can search for cultural events in your area or another city by date and performance type. There are also listings for international events.

- Culturefinder Allstars is the place to go to find "stats" on famous art, classical music, dance, opera, and theater craftspeople. If you are thinking about buying a classical music CD, but want more information before you make the purchase, click on Cultural Briefs.

- There is a dictionary for looking up basic arts terms, a full listing of summer festival schedules, arts magazine contacts, culture links to other relevant sites on the Web, composer biographies, and program notes.

Other Sites

Alvin Ailey American Dance Theater Home Page
http://www.alvinailey.org/

- The Alvin Ailey American Dance Theater is a world-renowned dance company. Visit this site to see photos and reviews of dances from the current Ailey repertoire, download a video clip, and learn more about the organization.

Smithsonian Institution
http://www.si.edu/

- The Smithsonian Institution houses over sixteen museums with more than 140 million artifacts and specimens. With links to each of the museums as well as general information about the Institution itself, the Smithsonian site is the granddaddy of all culture sites on the Web.

Theatre Central
http://www.theatre-central.com/

- If you are an avid theatergoer or just have a casual interest, go to the Theatre Central site to keep abreast of all things related to the theater.

News Sites

◆ **The New York Times on the Web** ◆ **CNN Interactive** ◆ **Other Sites**

If you are interested in keeping up-to-date on the day's top stories, check out the newspapers available to you online. In addition to fast-breaking news, you can check out feature articles on fashion, movies, political cartoons, and more. There's no need to buy a paper or wait for a television newscast when you can get up-to-the-minute information online 24-hours a day.

The New York Times on the Web

http://www.nytimes.com/

"All the news That's Fit to Print" is posted by these news distribution giants. Updated every 10 minutes, the New York Times site brings you all the news, all the time.

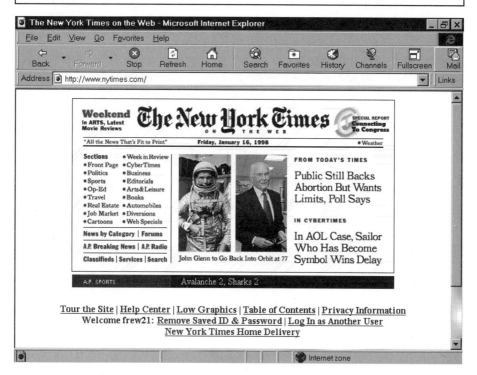

- To begin using this mammoth site, you must first register. Registering is free and takes approximately 2 minutes to complete. Once you've registered, select a news section, such as Front Page or Sports, click on a headline to read an article, or click on News by Category to see headings that include international, national, metro, style, arts, and a photo gallery. From most articles you can access related articles and/or online forums. From Front Page you can click to read quick summaries of the day's top news stories.

- Click on CyberTimes to access all breaking technological news as well as past articles. This page also posts an excellent Internet glossary and guide and other news, views, and resources that deal with the electronic age.

- The New York Times site can be searched by today's articles or by all articles, which includes the CyberTimes.

- If you use Netscape Navigator as your browser, you can sign up for the free service New York Times Direct. This free service will daily deliver content from selected sections directly to your Netscape mailbox. Register for this feature by selecting Services from the home page, and then select the options under The New York Times Direct.

- If you are running Internet Explorer 4, you can include the New York Times as one of your channels. You can also have New York Times content broadcast directly to your desktop.

- For up-to-the-minute news, select AP Breaking News for the hottest stories. The features on this page are updated every 10 minutes.

- When you get tired of the news, select Diversions to test your knowledge on the Times' trivia quiz or view cartoons online. Also, if you are an at-home Times subscriber or are willing to pay $9.95, you can subscribe to the Premium Diversions service, which provides crossword puzzles, chess, and bridge columns.

CNN Interactive

http://www.cnn.com/

Get all the news you need from the worldwide leader in cable television news. You can also access more than 100 other sources, including CNN online services such as CNNsi, which is a collaboration between CNN and Sports Illustrated.

- The CNN cable news network is widely recognized as the world leader in news reporting, so it makes sense that the CNN Interactive Web site should be as feature and content rich as the 24-hour news network's television coverage.

- The CNN Interactive site brings together the resources of CNN's own newsgathering team and the content of more than 100 other magazines and news outlets.

- The CNN Interactive home page presents the day's headlines with links to full stories. Also available from the very long home page is a menu bar where you can click on news topics of interest, including World, U.S., Local, Weather, Sports, Sci-Tech, Style, Travel, Showbiz, Health, and Earth.

- Links to other CNN online services from the home page include CNNfn for financial and business news, CNNSI for sports news, and allpolitics for political coverage.

- Scroll down the home page to view a complete directory of CNN Interactive site links, including direct links to stories under the main heading categories noted above.

- If the sheer volume of available news at this site is a little overwhelming, click on the Custom News link near the top of the home page. This link takes you to a page where you can register free of charge to customize the CNN Interactive page to suit your news needs.

- Select the Video Vault to download and view videos of current happenings. You can also take CNN's news quiz to see if you are up on your current events.

- From the Video Vault pages click on the CNNPlus link to see a page devoted to personal features and news about topics such as Consumer, Community, Games, and Resources. Click on the Local link from the menu bar of any page to get local news updates from CNN network affiliate TV stations in your city.

- From the CNNPlus page you can subscribe to Special Delivery, the weekly e-mail update for CNN Interactive users. This service e-mails you special CNN Interactive sections, information on technological breakthroughs, resources, CNN programming highlights, and more.

Other Sites
MSNBC
http://www.msnbc.com
- Quickly scan daily news headlines and read the news you need in more detail. This site also provides access to CNBC, MSNBC, and NBC television news.

International Herald Tribune
http://www.iht.com/IHT/home.html
- A true world newspaper, the International Herald Tribune's Web site is a great place to keep on top of world events.

NewsWorks
http://www.newsworks.com
- Get the day's news from more than 130 major U.S. newspaper Web sites.

Medical Advice

◆ Mayo Health Oasis ◆ Dental ResourceNet ◆ Other Sites

The number of sites containing medical advice and resource information is growing rapidly. The sites are getting better and the information more accessible. Now you can get information on nutrition, prenatal care, hundreds of common first aid solutions, and much more. You can also find information on more complex medical conditions such as cancer and diabetes.

Mayo Health Oasis

http://www.mayohealth.org/

Health, nutrition, and simple cures for ailments—it's all here at the Mayo Health Oasis. Click on the many links to different medical areas for valuable, free medical information.

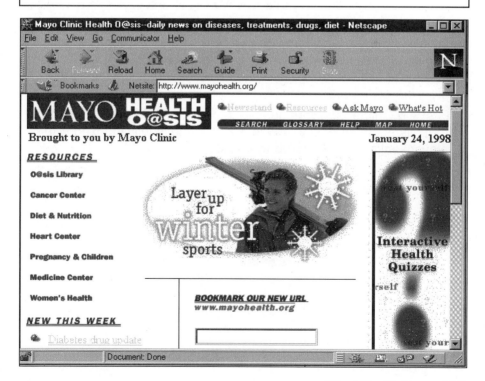

- The Mayo Health Oasis reflects the overall excellence you would expect from the highly esteemed Mayo Clinic. This easy-to-navigate site provides simple answers to a wide range of medical questions—from easy to complex. Furthermore, the information is presented in a casual, conversational tone.

- The Mayo Health Oasis has information on everything from advances in cancer research to health and nutrition to women's health.

- The Heart Center has answers to questions you may have about the positive and negative effects of aerobic activity, normal heart rate, pacemakers, and other heart-related issues.

- Each Resource Center topic includes links to several other pages. Click the link to "Ask the Mayo Physician" for answers by Mayo Clinic Physicians to questions sent in by anyone with a computer and an inquiry.

- The "Quiz" link provides a series of short, multiple-choice questions to test your knowledge on a specific resource topic. After taking the quick test, this interactive page allows you to check your answers and provides brief but informative material on each question asked.

- The other two Resource links—Reference Articles and Other Sites—connects you to relevant Mayo Clinic resource articles and other valuable Web sites.

- The Mayo Health Oasis has its own Newsstand and Library for reading articles and researching a variety of health topics. Click on the What's Hot link to find information on new medical topics that affect our daily lives.

- "First Aid Online" answers questions on what to do about everything from blisters to sprains to shock. Each listing is fully indexed with relevant links provided for further research.

- Many of the areas at the Mayo Health Oasis are updated on a daily basis, so check it often.

Dental ResourceNet

http://www.dentalcare.com

How much do you know about proper dental care? A good way to find out is to visit this site. Everything essential to proper dental care and dental procedures can be found here.

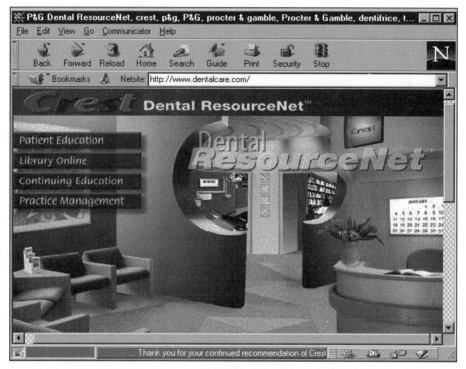

- The P&G Crest Dental ResourceNet answers the most common questions about effective dental care. It is important to point out that many areas on this site are primarily for the use of health care professionals and you must register as a professional to access this information. There are, however, informative areas that are available to lay people.

- While going to the dentist may be a frightening proposition and the idea of reading up on dental care even more so, this site makes the most out of what may at first seem unappealing. Click on the Patient Education link to learn more about such topics as proper dental hygiene, wisdom tooth treatments, and root canals.

- Click on the Consumer Site link at the bottom of the home page to go to the P&G House Call area. This area covers dental care for both adults and children. There are several pages with information on everything from the effects of smoking on your teeth to certain clinical disorders that can be detected in the dentist's chair. Be sure to check out the pages that outline how to choose a family dentist.

- Of course, Proctor and Gamble is in the business of selling products for your teeth, and you can find detailed information on their many dental products. Although this is a commercial site, Proctor and Gamble is very careful to keep the focus on consumer dental concerns and keeps its own commercial concerns to a minimum.

Other Sites

MedAccess

http://www.medaccess.com/

- MedAccess is among the best online medical resource sites on the Web. Here you can find links to the nation's best healthcare facilities as well as health and wellness topics and comprehensive healthcare information for senior citizens.

AllerDays Online

http://www.allerdays.com/

- Go to this site to find the causes of allergies and how to find relief. There are also pollen reports, the latest on allergy therapy and medications, and a forum where allergy sufferers share their allergy horror and relief stories.

National Institute of Mental Health's Anxiety Disorders

http://www.nimh.nih.gov/anxiety

- The National Institute of Mental Health's Anxiety Disorders Education Program is a national education campaign dedicated to educating public and health care professionals about how to identify anxiety disorders and their effective treatments.

Yahoo! Health Topic Search Site

http://www.yahoo.com/Health/

- Almost any health questions you have can be answered at this site. Questions on environmental health, transplant resources, or fitness can be answered by clicking on a link.

Law and Order

◆ **P-Law Legal Resource Locator** ◆ **West's Legal Directory** ◆ **Other Sites**

How many jokes have you heard about lawyers? However, there are times when getting a lawyer is no joking matter. Some day your knowledge of the legal system and your rights as a citizen, a potential homeowner, or an accident victim may be absolutely essential to a successful resolution. These sites all deal with law and order.

P-Law Legal Resource Locator

http://www.dorsai.org/p-law/

 This site is a collection of links to law information, lawyers, and legal sites. The site is easy to understand and navigate, but still requires a bit of patience.

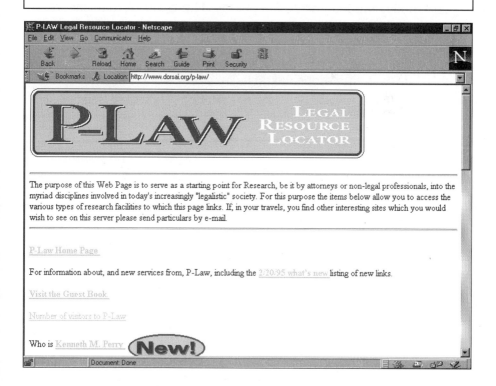

- The first thing to remember about lawyers is that they should be valued for their expertise and the enormous amount of time they have spent learning how to interpret the law. However, if you decide to test your own legal-eagle prowess, you can do a lot of legal research online. Such an endeavor requires time, effort, research, and resources. The P-Law Legal Resource Locator can help.

- Comprised of many different research sites, P-Law links you to online general law sites at major law universities. Click Specialized Topic Sites to go to sites with information on such topics as advertising, health, religious law, and social theory.

- The Legislative & Other Government Information Sites area offers links to government agency libraries, and other links that describe the government's role in writing and executing the law. Go to the U.S. Census Bureau for searchable government databases and the Library of Congress for copyright registrations and recorded copyright assignments information.

- Click the Miscellaneous Sites link to access West's Legal Dictionary or the ACLU Reading Room, which includes a collection of recent public policy reports and action guides. The Gallup Organization— an organization used to garner public opinion on various topics— can also be found in this area.

- P-Law is a law research site with no bells and whistles. It does, however, have numerous valuable links and a great deal of information that may help if you find yourself in need of legal assistance.

West's Legal Directory
http://www.wld.com/

 If you need advice on how to hire a lawyer or need to know the meaning of a legal term in a contract, read up on law topics from the West's Legal Directory.

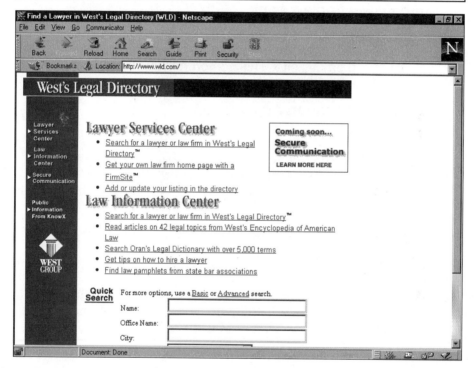

- This comprehensive directory covers it all—including a searchable database of over 800,000 lawyers, law articles, a law dictionary, an overview of the U.S. court system, and more.

- West's Legal Directory provides valuable tips on how to hire a lawyer. Click on Get tips on how to hire a lawyer for simple, legalese-free explanations of different types of lawyers and their specialties, the nature of law practices, where to find a lawyer, and the different types of fees that may be involved.

- The How to hire a lawyer page explains the nature of legal business in brief detail, starting with a list of questions that you might ask at the initial meeting. You can also learn about instances when you may not need counsel.

- The Law Information Center link provides quick, free information about lawyers and the law. Click these links to access information from legal articles, law dictionaries, tips on hiring a lawyer, and more.

Other Sites

Find Law Internet Resources

http://www.findlaw.com/

- Everything you always wanted to know about the law, the legal profession, the government, or becoming a lawyer can be found on this site. This comprehensive list is one of the greatest law resources on the Web.

American Arbitration Association

http://adr.org/

- American Arbitration Association is a nonprofit organization dedicated to resolving disputes using mediation, arbitration, negotiation, elections, and other methods of voluntary dispute resolution.

Comprehensive Legal and Business Form Library

http://www.mcn.net/~kerrlaw/

- This site contains hundreds of legal forms drafted by lawyers and put on diskette for your convenience. You can order the forms online using Visa or MasterCard.

Making the Move

◆ Relocation Central ◆ MoveQuest ◆ Other Sites

On the trauma meter, health professionals tell us that relocating is among the top three most stressful events in our lives. While the Internet can't help you with the psychological ordeal involved in moving, it can make the physical arrangements a little easier with Web sites that specialize in all areas of the moving process.

Relocation Central

http://relocationcentral.com/

 If you are about to move across the country or just across town, let Relocation Central help you make your move as stress-free as possible.

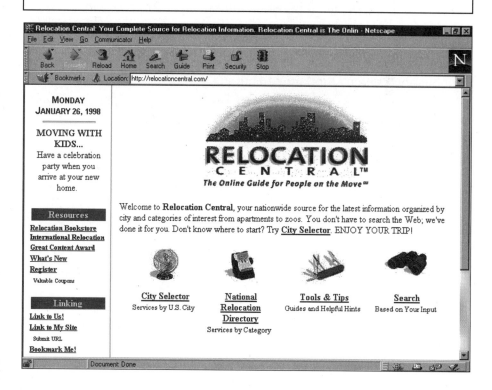

- Relocation Central bills itself as the most comprehensive relocation resource on the Web. They have compiled information from many different Web sources to make your online search easier.

- Details about the city where you plan to move, finding a home before or when you arrive, the job market, and basic city highlights for hundreds of cities across the country can be found here.

- Click on Tools & Tips for checklists, FAQs, calculators, chamber of commerce information, and more. Here you'll find the Relocation Wizard, which helps you develop a timeline or a moving plan for your move, and a Mover's Checklist. The checklist is helpful for remembering things like collecting medical records to take with you or remembering to notify old utility companies of your departure and the new companies of your arrival. The checklist may seem excessive, with over fifty items, but if even half the items help you organize your move, you'll be better off.

- The Moving Cost Calculator on the Tools & Tips page helps you compute Interstate moving costs. The costs are calculated based on the information you input about your current residence such as the number of furnished rooms, the amount of time you've lived there, and the distance between the old and new residence.

- If you plan to buy a new home, The Mortgage Calculator on the Tools & Tips page allows you to compute the loan amount for which you may qualify based on the debt and income information you input and certain standardized criteria.

- If you plan to rent, the Apartment Locator can put you in touch with several rental agencies in the desired area.

MoveQuest

http://www.movequest.com/

Not only does MoveQuest tell you how to make your move more efficient, but they also have links to help you save money on groceries and services in your new neighborhood.

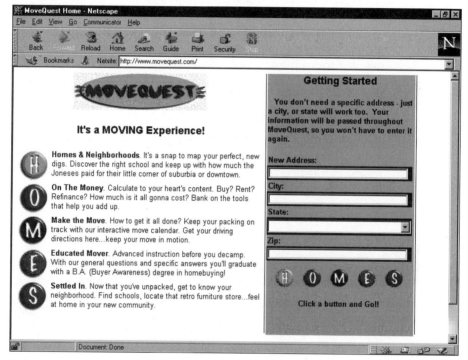

- MoveQuest has compiled more demographic information on hundreds of cities across the country than any other moving site. You can find out the average age of the people in the area where you want to live, crime statistics, the cost of the average house, the average apartment rental prices, and even see a map of the area.

- Moving to a new area can be very expensive, so any cost-cutting proposition is welcome. If you want food coupons and area merchant savings, then be sure to check out Hot Coupons. Click on the Settled In link from the MoveQuest menu on the right side of the screen and follow the H.O.T. Coupons links. It's very simple to use and the savings can add up.

- Click the Make the Move link to locate your local cable company, get driving directions, or use the Interactive Move Calculator to calculate moving expenses.

Other Sites

North American Van Lines

http://navl1.com/

- North American Van Lines offers several different moving options. You can choose complete moving services or you pack the stuff and they drive it to the final destination. Submit an online form with your contact information and moving details for more information.

State Farm Insurance

http://www.statefarm.com/

- State Farm is the largest property and casualty insurance agency. They offer auto, medical, natural disaster, and property insurance. Extensive online information is available about company and insurance policies.

Cort National Furniture Rental

http://www.cort1.com/

- If you are relocating for a short while and need home furnishings, Cort National Furniture Rental offers a full line of rental furnishings. Items include sofas, pots, pans, TVs, and VCRs. Complete the online form and select how you would like a representative to contact you directly.

The Handyman's Dream Sites

◆ **Home Improvement Net** ◆ **Better Homes and Gardens Home Page**
◆ **Other Sites**

"Good location. Close to schools and shopping. Priced to sell. Handyman special." Translation: *"Nice house. Needs work."* Now there is no need to pass up the deal of a lifetime because you don't know the first thing about home repairs. In many cases, you could be just a little plaster and a couple light fixtures away from your dream home.

Home Improvement Net

http://www.homeimprove.com

 Learn simple "how to" techniques from the Home Improvement Net to help you remodel, refurbish, and improve your home, lawn, and garden.

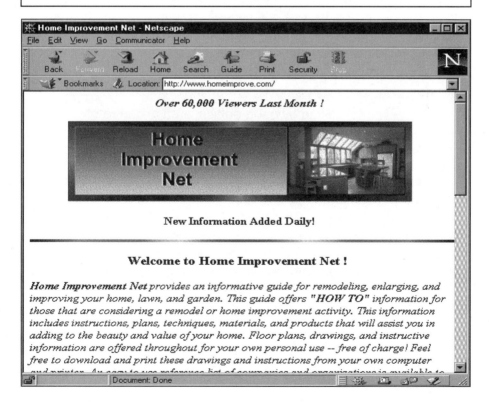

- Home Improvement Net is filled with "how to" instructions for remodeling home interiors, exteriors, putting in pools and spas, and even building a new home. They give you valuable information on how to deal with contractors and other home improvement personnel successfully. To explore this site, the first thing you must do is select a geographical area in the U.S. or Canada for a local edition of the site.

- For information on remodeling and designing home interiors, click the Interiors link from the local edition page. This section gives tips on planning room additions, staining wood floors, decorating a home office, and room furnishings like bathroom lighting and oriental rugs. They also discuss techniques for carpentry, painting, plumbing, and lighting. Just click the category of your choice.

- The Exteriors link from the local edition page discusses the best way to evaluate and maintain your home's exterior with a checklist of annual tasks. You can learn a variety of techniques, from how to detect when something is seriously wrong to how to create and maintain gardens, lawns, and plants.

- When dealing with contractors, it is a good idea to know as much as you can about permits and regulations. Click the Permits & Regs. link on the local edition page to learn more information and save a great deal of frustration in the long run.

- If you are remodeling an old house, click on "That Vintage Home" for methods specifically tailored to working on older structures.

- You'll find vendors listed by geographical area and area of concentration on virtually every page of Home Improvement Net. If you need to hire a professional to help with your home improvement project, click the Vendor state link at the bottom of any page to display lists of architects, engineers, contractors, lawyers, realtors, and financial lenders in your area.

- Shop for design and construction books and services by clicking the Product and Service Showcase link from the local edition page. From this area, you can purchase resource books on interior decorating, financing home improvement projects, installing an in-home security system, and other featured services.

Better Homes and Gardens Home Page
http://www.bhglive.com/index.shtml

 Better Homes and Gardens may be the most complete home improvement resource on the Web. Extensive home improvement tips are designed to save you time and money.

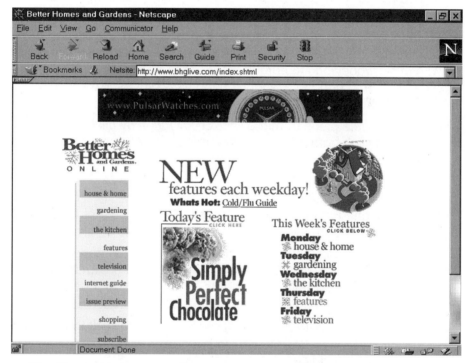

- The Better Homes and Gardens site is organized into ten major categories covering topics such as house and home, gardening, the kitchen, magazine and television highlights, special features, shopping, real estate services, and more.

- From the house & home page, click the Home Improvement Encyclopedia link to find over one hundred links to home improvement tips, techniques, advice, and information. And that's just the beginning. In total, there are over 1,000 home improvement tips and over 125 shockwave animations, all listed by category for easy access.

- From the Home Improvement Encyclopedia, click Home Improvement Basics to get helpful tips on handling home emergencies such as gas leaks and fires. In the Home Improvement Encyclopedia, you'll also find carpentry tips, plumbing and electrical information, landscaping techniques, an extensive tool dictionary, and project calculators.

- From the house & home page Home Forum, you can get seasonal decorating ideas, browse past articles from the archives, and share innovative home improvement ideas and techniques with other Better Homes and Gardens readers.

- From the house & home page, click the WOOD Online link for all your woodworking needs. There you can share tips and techniques with other woodworking enthusiasts, see project plans and blueprints, and purchase woodworking accessories like tool kits and books.

- Purchase home plans from the BH&G collection by clicking the Homeplans link from the house & home page. You can browse the BH&G collection or search for specific plans that meet your needs.

- If you are mulling over design options, check out the DesignerFinder page from the house & home page. The Traditional Home DesignerFinder service helps you find a decorator in your area, choose design styles, and calculate the costs involved.

- Once you have completed a few renovations and increased the value of your home, visit the BH&G buying & selling your home page to get tips on real estate agents in your area, mortgage services, effective marketing techniques, and relocation tips.

- If you're still looking for more resources, be sure to click the Internet guide link to explore favorite BH&G Internet sites from gardening to interior design, building, and remodeling.

Other Sites

Sound Home Resource Center

http://www.soundhome.com/

- Find hundreds of topics relevant to home construction, remodeling, and maintenance. This comprehensive site answers questions about home building and improvement, contains a glossary of terms, recommends books on relevant topics, and list links to other home improvement and construction sites.

Home Depot

http://www.homedepot.com/

- Home Depot is one of the leading retailers of home improvement and construction goods. They stock over 40,000 different kinds of materials, supplies, and gardening products. Click on the To Locate the Store Nearest You link to find a Home Depot in your area.

The Garden Gate

http://www.prairienet.org/ag/garden/homepage.htm

- Practically every link pertaining to gardening can be found on this site. Here you will find horticulture links to sites all over the world with helpful tips for creating a beautiful garden and caring for your indoor plants.

Net Pet Care

◆ AVMA Care for Pets ◆ Healthy Pets ◆ Other Sites

The positive affect our four-legged friends have on our daily lives is absolutely invaluable. If for no other reason, we owe it to our pets to learn how to care for them properly. Get online advice on the most effective ways to care for your pet from nutritional information to preventative health care to fun training techniques.

AVMA Care for Pets

http://www.avma.org/care4pets/

 Who better to know a pet than a vet? Whether you have a dog, cat, turtle, or horse, the American Veterinary Association has practical advice for effective pet care.

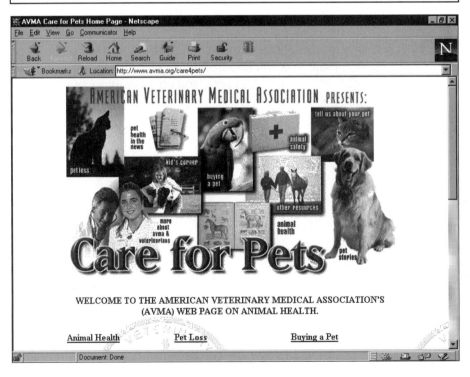

180

- It only makes sense that the Care for Pets site by the American Veterinary Medical Association is one of the best pet care sites on the Web. Each area contains brief but informative pages on everything from buying a pet to coping with the loss of a pet. The nine links at the bottom of each page take you to specific pet care areas.

- If you don't already have a pet, click on the Buying a Pet link to get advice on how to choose the right animal for you. This area also includes facts on how different kinds of animals are affected by their environment.

- Just as you might childproof your home for your child's safety, click on the Animal Safety link to find out how to petproof your home effectively. There is information on pet first aid, sanitation practices, effective interaction between kids and pets, and preventative techniques to avoid pet injury and illness inside and outside of the home.

- The Pet Health in the News page provides links to a variety of pet health tips. Here you can learn about preventative measures you can take insure your pet's good health, facts on proper dental care, vaccinations, common signs of illness, and various treatments.

- Among the other links located on this site, The Kids Korner contains activities for children with pets or a love of animals. Tell Us About Your Pet is a forum to share stories about your pet with other pet lovers, and Other Resources contains links to other Web pet care resources.

Healthy Pets

http://www.healthypet.com/

Dogs and cats are the most popular pet choices. As a result, this site is loaded with information on caring for these two animals. However, there is also information on birds and other small animals.

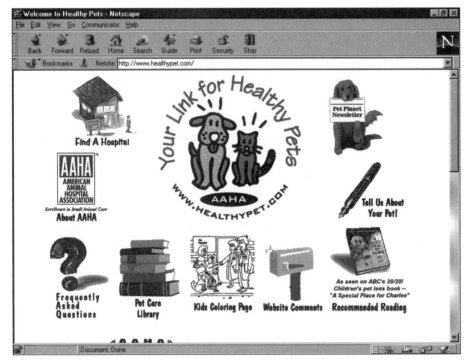

- The American Animal Hospital Association (AAHA) maintains this site, an organization of over 13,000 veterinarians. AAHA's message is basically that pets are important members of your family, so you should treat them as such. Proper care includes annual physical examinations, vaccinations, dental care, diet, and exercise. The Healthy Pets site deals with all of these topics and more.

- Go to the Pet Care Library for answers to health questions, animal behavior, and the best training methods for your pet. There are training hints for housetraining puppies and litter box training cats. There is also information on preventing bad behavior in dogs and cats.

- Click on Find A Hospital to locate an AAHA-accredited veterinary hospital anywhere in the United States or Canada. From the Hospital page you can also access and complete a first-aid chart for your pet. This chart has life-saving tips on what to do in a pet emergency.

- The Pet Planet Newsletter is updated bi-monthly and covers a variety of topics. For example, the winter issue focused on dry skin. Like people, pets' skin needs a little extra attention when it's cold outside and the heat is turned up high inside.

Other Sites

Healthy Paws

http://healthypaws.com/index.html

- If you love your pet and are willing to spend a little cash, you have to go to this site. Purchase a variety of things for your animal from dog sweaters to pearl necklaces for your cat. Facts on pet vitamins as well as general heath can also be found here.

Animal Related Laws

http://merkury.saic.com/ranger/shelters/legal.html

- Read up on restraint and leash laws, dog licenses, and the laws regarding humane animal care. This information is slightly altered or reworded from the San Diego County Code, but the laws and their interpretations presented here are true for most county codes concerning animals.

Delta Society

http://www2.deltasociety.org/deltasociety/

- The Delta Society mission statement is "To promote animals helping people improving their health, independence and quality of life." At this site you will find information on the positive psychological effects animals have on people, animal-assisted therapy, and trained service dogs for the disabled.

Job Sites Online

◆ **Monster Board Career Search** ◆ **CareerPath** ◆ **Other Sites**

When you want to look for a job you need not rely solely on the Sunday newspaper. The Internet contains hundreds of job sites featuring job listings as well as other career management information. Listed below and on the following pages are some of the Internet's best.

Monster Board Career Search

http://www.monster.com/

With 50,000 job listings per day, Monster Board Career Search is the largest of the Internet's job sites.

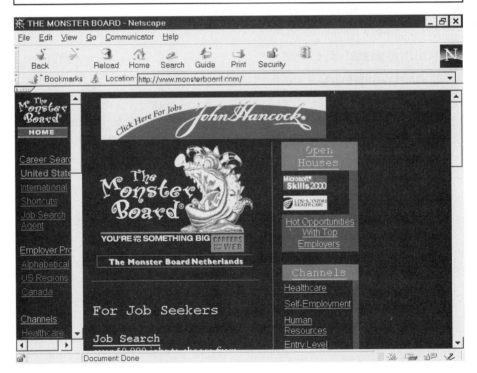

- Monster Board is the online job site of choice for people who want job information with an edge. The monster theme carries throughout, including the monster characters Thwacker, who "has compiled a monstrous list of U.S. career opportunities with more than 7,000 progressive employers," and Swoop, who "is a tireless monster that will zero in on perfect job matches, dive in and grab them, then deliver them" to you even when you are offline.

- Swoop, your personal job search agent, is a terrific resource. Once you have created a profile with Monster Board, Swoop will send job listings that match your profile to either your Profile In Box or to your e-mail address. You do not need to be online or reenter your criteria. Swoop does the work for you. And, best of all, the service is free.

- The database of jobs can be searched by discipline, location, or keywords and phrases. You can also search for either full-time or part-time employment. In addition, you can post your resume so that employers or recruiters can contact you.

- Use the Resume Builder to create an online resume. To create the resume you need to provide information, both fill in the blank and short answer, and then the builder formats the resume for you. Once you have created the resume you can apply to any of the job listings. You can always go back to edit or change your posted resume. (See sites under "Resume Resources" for more information on building a solid resume.)

CareerPath

http://careerpath.com

One of the most efficient and extensive job listing and career resources sites. You can search classified ad listings and leading industry employers. You can also post your resume so that employers can contact you.

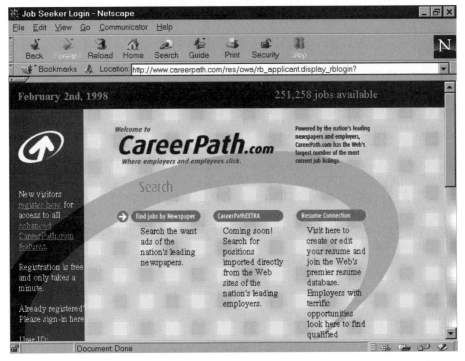

- The CareerPath Web site is simple and well organized and all the services are free. Take advantage of setting up an account with CareerPath so that you only need to enter your search criteria once.

- There are two databases for job seekers to search. The Find Jobs by Newspaper database is compiled from the classified ads of 30 different newspapers. The search criteria are based on keywords, job type, or location. On any given day the job bank contains nearly 200,000 job listings.

- The Employer Profiles database contains information about leading industry employers. Before you go on any job interviews, be sure to check this database to see if you can obtain information on the organization with which you plan to interview. Nothing impresses an interviewer more than an interviewee who has done her or his homework.

- The resume connection is a step-by-step service you can use to create an online resume. Once you have all your education and job experience handy, creating the resume is easy. When your resume is complete, it is added to the site's resume database. Personal information, such as your name and phone number, is not released to the potential employer until you read the job description and give CareerPath the OK to release any identifying information.

- Click on Career Resources for expert information on interview strategies, resume tips, networking pointers, and more.

- The streamlined interface of the CareerPath site makes navigating simple, efficient, and user-friendly.

Other Sites

Career Starters

http://www.asaenet.org/aboutasae/jobservices/cstarter.html

- This site lists entry positions with salaries up to $30,000.

CareerBuilder

http://careerbuilder.com

- A comprehensive job site with excellent career advice and such features as a free service that searches for job sites that match your criteria.

Online Career Center

http://www.occ.com

- This award-winning site was the first job clearinghouse page on the Web. Excellent career resources and easy-to-use job database searching make this site worth visiting.

E-Span

http://www.espan.com

- This site provides more in-depth screening services for both employers and job seekers to ensure that the right person is matched to the right job. There are fewer job listings here than at other sites, but greater selectivity in the screening process means a better chance of finding what you want.

Resume Resources

◆ **Kaplan's Career Center: Resume Styles**
◆ **JobSmart: Resumes & Cover Letters** ◆ **Other Sites**

When you send a potential employer your resume and cover letter, most often that—and that alone—is what you will be judged on. A lot is riding on those few pages. Your resume is representing you, so don't just throw something together. A good resume is the only way that you can secure an interview. Give your resume a lot of thought, show it to friends or family for feedback, be sure to *always* spell check, and explore the resume resources that are available to you online.

Kaplan's Career Center: Resume Styles

http://www.kaplan.com/career/Resume.html

 Kaplan, a dependable name in educational services, also maintains sites that are career related. The information posted on the resume and cover letter pages helps you make a good first impression.

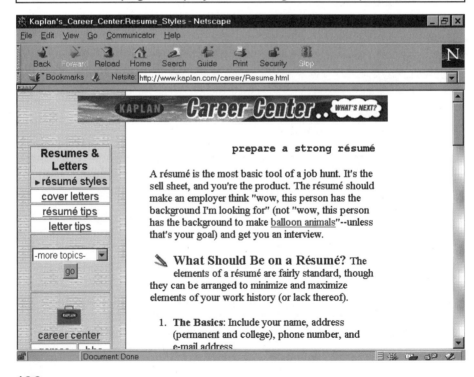

- When you build or update your resume, you don't want to tell the reader the story of your life. You just want to say enough to get an interview with your potential new employer. The home page for the Kaplan's resume styles lists just the basics for both content and style.

- Start by reading through What Should be on a Resume? This section simply lists the 7 critical elements that you should include in any resume. A brief paragraph under each topic describes the ingredients that go into each section.

- Click on resume tips or Resume Tips-a-go-go for ten rules of the resume road, such as make your resume look good and avoid gimmicks.

- If your cover letter (which you must *always* include) is not well prepared there is a chance that the reviewer will not even get to your resume. Be sure to click on the cover letters link to see what a cover letter should and should not contain. At the bottom of this page, the link to Cover Letter Tips-a-go-go lists the ten dos and don'ts for preparing your cover letter.

- The Career Center link opens the door to the Kaplan Career Center home page. From this site, you can click to view a resume filled with mistakes to see if you can catch the errors. You can then see the resume, using the same basic information, done properly. This is an excellent exercise and should definitely be checked out. The same activity is also supplied using a cover letter.

- On the Career Center home page you can click on The Hot Seat: Wacky Job Interview Game. In this game you must respond to an interviewer's questions and try to get the job. If you select the wrong answer, you loose the game and the job.

- The Career Center also posts career tips, feature articles, and suggestions on how to deal with job-interview stress.

JobSmart: Resumes & Cover Letters
http://jobsmart.org/tools/resume/index.htm

The JobSmart resume resources supports the idea that resumes are like shoes; one style is not right for everyone. Depending on your work or educational experience and what type of job you are looking for, there are different resume formats that may better suit your needs.

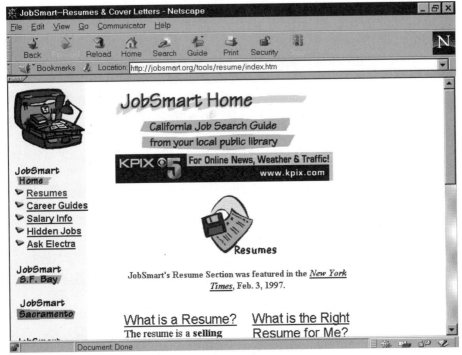

- After reading the basic information under What is a Resume?, click on What is the Right Resume for Me? to get started. The four formats that are listed are chronological, functional (recommended for new graduates with not a lot of experience), curriculum vitae, and electronic (for posting your resume on online sites). You can view samples of both the chronological and functional resumes.

- Click on Selected Resume Resources on the Web to get to links to Yahoo!'s collection of resume resources (many of which are worth while), as well as links to general resources, first job resources, recent graduate resources, and others.

190

- The resume tips that are provided from Yana Parker are solid, and many of the strategies that she suggests are relevant for people who have already had work experience.

- The Cover Letters link *must* be accessed. The material on this page stresses the importance of taking the extra time to prepare a complete and well-written letter. There is also information on the elements needed to create a good cover letter, things you should avoid, sample letters, and resources. Remember that you never get a second chance to make a first impression.

- Ask Electra (who is really a librarian with an ordinary name) is a service of JobSmart where you can e-mail job or career questions which are then posted and answered. Many of the questions that are featured here were written by people who have had years and years of experience in the job market, but you will also find some questions written by high school students who are about to join the workforce.

Other Sites

Writing a Winning Resume and Cover Letter
http://www.gov.calgary.ab.ca/81/next/81yecpa1.htm

- This is a fun and informative site. Start by testing your resume IQ and then move on to what to include and what to omit when writing your resume. The 12 quick tips that are listed and the cartoon illustrations are right on target.

JobWeb: Resume Writing Tips
http://www.jobweb.org/catapult/guenov/restips.html

- This site provides resume basics and guides you through the steps of building a solid resume.

Resume Proofreading Checklist
http://www.careermosaic.com/cm/11online/11online7.html

- Print out this list and go through it before you send your resume out to prospective employers.

Rebecca Smith's eResumes and Resources
http://www.eresumes.com/

- This is an online guide that walks you through the steps of preparing an electronic resume. Includes information on creating electronic cover letters and posting the resume and letter once complete.

Appendix A: Essential Downloads

The Internet can be a convenient source for downloading valuable software. Log on to the following URLs to download Web and multimedia software, much of which is available free of charge or as shareware, which requires a minimal registration fee.

Internet Explorer

http://www.microsoft.com/ie/download/

- Internet Explorer 4.0 is the latest version of Microsoft's Internet browser software. It has attracted a lot of attention for both it's powerful new features and it's role in the Department of Justice investigation of Microsoft for antitrust violations.

- Explorer 4.0's active desktop features allow the browser software to be much more integrated into the Windows operating system you use to run your computer.

- You can also receive active content from the Web using Explorer's "push" technology. Active content lets you choose from among several Web content "channels" to receive automatic information updates to your desktop.

- Other Explorer 4.0 tools include NetMeeting virtual conferencing software and FrontPage Express. NetMeeting helps facilitate virtual meetings held via the Internet and one-to-one telephone calls from your computer. FrontPage Express enables you to create and post your own Web pages.

- Whatever the outcome of the legal wrangling, Explorer is rapidly gaining market acceptance as the leading Web browser. Get your copy free of charge at this site.

Netscape Navigator

http://home.netscape.com/download/index.html

- Netscape Navigator 4.0 is the other major Web browser on the market today and the direct descendant of the Mosaic browser that first swept many users into the world of surfing the Web.

- Netscape Communicator includes Navigator 4.0 and a complete suite of Internet tools, including Messenger for e-mail, Collabra for newsgroups, and Composer for creating Web pages.

- You can also download a complete installation of Netscape Communicator which includes Netscape Netcaster for receiving active channel content, Netscape Conference for online collaboration and the capability to handle rich multimedia content as well as bitstream fonts.

- Though you must pay for Netscape products available at this download site, you can download evaluation versions of new software free of charge. Educational institutions and nonprofit organizations can download a number of Netscape products at no charge.

TUCOWS

http://www.tucows.com

- TUCOWS stands for The Ultimate Collection Of Winsock Software. The site bills itself as the world's best collection of Internet software.

- After logging on to the TUCOWS home page, click the appropriate link for your geographical location (such as United States, Europe, Canada), then click the appropriate state (or other area) link. These geographical links are used to produce faster and more reliable software downloads.

- Next click the appropriate link for your computer's operating system. You will see a directory page listing links for more than 60 different types of Internet software.

- Click on a category link to see a listing of software available in that category for downloading. Listings include a complete description of the software, its hardware requirements, and a rating of the software (by number of cows). Click the Download button next to a particular listing to start downloading.

- Most software available at TUCOWS is either shareware or freeware, though some products offered are only demo versions that may have limited features or time restraints.

Shareware.Com

http://www.shareware.com

- Shareware.Com is another great site for downloading software via the Web. The site is a service of the C/Net Web page, noted for its computer and technology news coverage.

- You can browse the site by clicking on the New Arrivals or Most Popular links, or you can simply enter the name of the software you hope to find in the search engine text box.

- Highlights of available shareware are shown on the home page. Click on a link to go to a description of the shareware and a link to the download page.

The Jumbo Download Network

http://www.jumbo.com

- Yet another great software downloading site is The Jumbo Download Network, which lists more than 250,000 shareware programs and links. Available software is conveniently organized by channels, including Business, Desktop, Internet, Utilities, Games, Entertainment, Developer, and Demo City, which offers the latest commercial demos so you can try before you buy.

VDOLive Video Player

http://www.vdo.net/download/

- Download VDOnet Corporation's VDOLive Video Player 3.0 free of charge at this site. VDOLive is the top software for broadcasting and receiving video content over the Internet and is used by many major television networks, including CBS News, MTV, and PBS.

- Click on the VDOLive 3.0 link to begin downloading the software. You must register to download, but otherwise the procedure is free and relatively easy. Only the VDOLive Player software is available for free download. VDOLive server software must be purchased.

- You can also download a trial version of VDOPhone, touted as the first full-color video telephone available for either regular telephone lines or the Internet. VDOPhone lets you see and hear anyone over the Internet with no additional phone charges.

- VDOPhone is currently available for Windows 95 users only. The trial version expires after 5 hours of video reception.

Adobe Acrobat Reader

http://www.adobe.com

- Adobe Acrobat Reader lets you view, navigate, and print many document files available on the Web for downloading.

- To download the Acrobat Reader free of charge, click the Free Plug-Ins and Updates link at the Adobe home page. The link takes you to a file library page that displays a list of nearly thirty software products you can download. Links to download sites for each type of software are displayed by operating system.

- Click the Acrobat Reader link for your computer's operating system. The reader is available for Windows, Macintosh, DOS, UNIX, and OS/2. You will go to a page including short description links and download links for the available versions of Acrobat Reader. Click the Download link to register and begin downloading.

- You can also click the Tryout Software link at the Adobe home page to see descriptions of Adobe's latest multimedia and graphics products as well as download links for trial versions.

Shockwave

http://www.macromedia.com/shockwave/download/

- Macromedia Shockwave facilitates smooth viewing of animation and multimedia over the Internet. Many Web browsers and online services such as Internet Explorer, Netscape Navigator, and AOL include Shockwave with their software.

- If you want to download Shockwave, go to the Shockwave Download Center at the above URL, and click the Get Shockwave link.

Appendix B: Timesaving Tools

◆ Financial Calculators ◆ Calculators Online
◆ Universal Currency Converter ◆ The Time Zones Page ◆ Naval Clock
◆ Fast Area Code Finder ◆ National Address and Zip+4 Browser

Use the Web tools listed here to save time by finding the answer to many common financial and mathematical questions. You can also get the correct time around the world with the Time Zones and Naval Clock sites.

Financial Calculators

http://www.moneyadvisor.com/calc/

- Have you ever wondered whether you should lease or purchase a car? How much money do you have to save to become a millionaire by the time you retire? How much rent can you afford?

- The financial calculators available at the Financial Calculators page of the TimeValue Software Web site provide a host of interesting and practical tools for finding the answer to your financial questions.

- The directory of calculator links includes categories such as Auto Loans & Leasing, Loans & Savings Calculators, General Financial Calculators, Mortgage Calculators, Insurance Calculators, Tax Calculators, and Just For Fun Calculators.

Calculators Online

http://www-sci.lib.uci.edu/HSG/RefCalculators.html

- Another calculator site at Martindale's "The Reference Desk" provides more than 5,300 calculators.

- Links to the calculators are arranged in an alphabetical index of categories and subtopics. Click on a link to use one of the calculators.

- Business categories include Home & Office, Finance, Management/Business, Insurance, Stocks, Bonds, Options, and Commodities & Futures.

- You can also find many calculators for practical matters such as clothing, arts and crafts, medical, and law. Numerous mathematics and science calculators are also available, from simple unit conversion calculators to astrophysics.

Universal Currency Converter

http://www.xe.net./currency/

- This simple and useful Web site does one thing only, but does it well—currency conversion. If, for example, you want to know how many French francs you can get for $100, turn to this Web page.
- Type the amount of currency you want to convert, then select the type of currency (e.g., U.S. dollars). Next, select the type of currency you're converting to (e.g., French francs), and click the Perform Currency Conversion button.
- The Currency Converter tells you that $100 converts to 596.90 French francs. (Note that currency exchange rates fluctuate and converting currency usually requires a fee.)

The Time Zone Page

http://www.west.net/~lindley/zone/

- Another simple but very useful site is the Time Zone Page. Find the current time for more than 600 cities around the world.
- Select a city from the menu, then click Get the Time!

Naval Clock

http://tycho.usno.navy.mil/cgi-bin/timer.pl

- To check the most accurate clock available, go to the Naval Clock Web site. The site displays the current time in all North American time zones as well as Universal Time (also called Greenwich Mean Time).

Fast Area Code Finder

http://www.555-1212.com/aclookup.html

- Find an area code fast at this handy site. Simply enter a city name and/or click on a state from the drop-down list menu, then click Get Area Code! If you know the area code but want to find where the code serves, type the area code in the Area Code text box and click Get Location.

National Address and ZIP+4 Browser

http://www.semaphorecorp.com/cgi/form.html

- If you need to look up a Zip Code, go to this site and enter the company name plus as much of its address as you know. The Zip Browser returns the complete, correct address, including the correct 9-digit Zip Code. Great for cleaning up old mailing lists.

Appendix C: Viruses

Introduction

- Viruses are malicious programs written to attempt some form of deliberate destruction to someone's computer. They are instructions or code that have been written to reproduce as they attach themselves to other programs without the user's knowledge. Viruses can be programmed to do anything a computer can do. Viruses are a nuisance, but if you know how they work and take the necessary precautions to deal with them, they are manageable. It is essential that you understand the nature of these programs, how they work, and how they can be disinfected. No one is exempt from viruses; strict precautions and anti-virus programs are the answer.

- Viruses are potentially destructive to one file or to an entire hard disk, whether the file or hard disk is one used in a standalone computer or in a multi-user network. Like biological viruses, computer viruses need a host, or a program, to infect. Once infection has been transferred, the viruses can spread like wildfire through the entire library of files. Like human sickness, viruses come in many different forms; some are more debilitating than others.

Origins of Viruses

- How do you get a virus? They can come from a couple of places:
  - An infected diskette
  - Downloading an infected file from a bulletin board, the Internet, or an online service
- Knowing where viruses are likely to be introduced will make you sensitive to the possibility of getting one.

198

Categories of Viruses

- Viruses come in two categories:
  - Boot Sector Viruses
  - File Viruses

- **Boot Sector Viruses** may also be called System Sector viruses because they attack the system sector. System or boot sectors contain programs that are executed when the PC is booted. System or boot sectors do not have files. The hardware reads information in the area in the bootup sections of the computer. Because these sectors are vital for PC operation, they are prime target areas for viruses.

- Two types of system sectors exist: DOS sectors and partition sectors. PCs characteristically have a DOS sector and one or more sectors created by the partitioning command, FDISK, or proprietary partitioning software. Partition sectors are commonly called Master Boot Records (MBR). Viruses that attach to these areas are seriously damaging ones.

- **File Viruses** are more commonly found. Characteristically, a file virus infects by overwriting part or all of a file.

Timing of Viruses

- Viruses come in many sizes and with various symptoms. For example, a virus may attach itself to a program immediately and begin to infect an entire hard disk. Or the virus can be written to attack at a specific time. For example, the Michelangelo virus strikes on his birthday each May.

- Some viruses are written so that they delay letting you know of their existence until they have done major damage.

Virus Symptoms

- How can you tell if you have a virus? Hopefully, you will install anti-virus software in your PC that will identify viruses and make you aware immediately upon entry to your system. Otherwise, you may experience different symptoms such as:
  - Slow processing
  - Animation or sound appearing out of nowhere
  - Unusually heavy disk activity
  - Odd changes in files
  - Unusual printer activity

Precautions

- Most viruses spread when you have booted the computer from an infected diskette. A healthy precaution here would be to boot only from the hard drive.

  - Backup all files. At least two complete backups are recommended.

  - Even new software can come with a virus; scan every diskette before use.

  - Mark all software program attributes as read only.

  - Research and update anti-virus products on an ongoing basis to have the latest protection.

  - Since there are many types of viruses, one type of anti-virus protection won't disinfect all viruses. The safest approach is to install a multiple anti-virus program library.

Appendix D: Emoticons and Abbreviations

Since you cannot see the people with whom you communicate on the Internet, here are some symbols you can use to convey emotion in your messages. This section also contains some acronyms that you will encounter in Internet messages (such as e-mail, newsgroup messages, and chat room discussions). Be sure to use these cute symbols and abbreviations *only* in your personal communications.

For more emoticons and acronyms, go to the Emoticons & Smileys page:

http://home.earthlink.net/~gripweeds/emoticon.htm

Emoticons

- Use these symbols to convey emotions in your messages. To see the faces in these symbols, turn the page to the right.

>:->	Angry	:-(	Sad
5:-)	Elvis	:-@	Scream
:-)	Happy	:-#	Secret (lips are sealed)
()	Hug	:P	Sticking Tongue Out
:-D	Joking	:-O	Surprised
:*	Kiss	:-J	Tongue in Cheek
:/)	Not Funny	;-)	Wink

Acronyms

- Listed below are some of the more-common acronyms, but new acronyms are always being created. Be sure to check online to see what's new.

ADN	Any day now	**GMTA**	Great minds think alike
ASAP	As soon as possible	**IAE**	In any event
B4N	Bye for now	**IMO**	In my opinion
BRB	Be right back	**IRL**	In real life
BTW	By the way	**JIC**	Just in case
DTRT	Do the right thing	**LOL**	Laugh out loud
F2F	Face to face	**ROTFL**	Rolling on the floor laughing
FAQ	Frequently asked questions	**RTM**	Read the manual
FWIW	For what it's worth	**TIA**	Thanks in advance
FYI	For your information	**WFM**	Works for me

Appendix E: Netiquette

Netiquette is the art of civilized communications between people on the Internet. Whenever you send an e-mail message, a chat room message, or a newsgroup message follow these guidelines.

A Few Tips

- Always include a subject in the message heading. This makes it easy for the recipient to organize messages in folders by topic and to find a message by browsing through message headers.
- Do not use capital letters. To the recipient, it feels like YOU ARE SHOUTING. Instead, enclose text that you want to emphasize with asterisks. For example: I *meant* Friday of *next* week.
- Be careful with the tone you use. With the absence of inflection, it is easy to send a message that can be misinterpreted by the recipient. Use emoticons to establish your intent. A smiley emoticon can make it clear to the recipient that you are really joking.
- Spell check your messages before you send them. They represent you.
- Do not send flame messages. These are obnoxious, offensive, or otherwise disturbing messages. If you send this type of message to a newsgroup, 30,000 people who read your flame will think less of you. If you receive flame mail, probably the best thing you can do is press the Delete button rather than the Reply button.
- Messages sent over the Internet are not private. Your message is in writing and nothing can prevent someone from forwarding it to anyone they please. Assume that anyone with a computer has the potential to read your message.
- If you send a long message, it is a good idea to tell the recipient at --1,0the beginning of the message so that they can decide if they would rather download it to read fs.
- Never initiate or forward a chain letter. Some service providers will cancel your membership if you do so, as they are trying to protect their members from unwanted mail.

The Netiquette Home Page
http://www.albion.com/netiquette/index.html

- This page lists hyperlinks to pages on Netiquette contributed by Internet users. You will find interesting, amusing, and very important material in these sites.

Glossary

Listed below and on the following pages are terms that you may encounter on your Internet travels.

address book A place where frequently used e-mail addresses are stored.

anonymous FTP A special kind of FTP service that allows any user to log on. Anonymous FTP sites have a predefined user named "anonymous" that accepts any password.

Archie A database system of FTP resources. It helps you find files that exist anywhere on the Internet.

ARPAnet (Advanced Research Projects Administration Network)
Ancestor to the Internet: ARPAnet began in 1969 as a project developed by the US Department of Defense. Its initial purpose was to enable researchers and military personnel to communicate in the event of an emergency.

ASCII file (American Standard Code for Information Interchange) File containing ASCII-formatted text only; can be read by almost any computer or program in the world.

attachment File(s) or Web pages(s) enclosed with an e-mail message.

Base64 (MIME) encoding One of the encoding schemes, used in the MIME (Multipurpose Internet Mail Extensions) protocol.

binary file A file containing machine language (that is, ones and zeros) to indicate that the file is more than plain text. A binary file must be encoded (converted to ASCII format) before it can be passed through the e-mail system.

BinHex An encoding scheme for the Macintosh platform that allows a file to be read as text when passed through the e-mail system.

bookmark A browser feature that memorizes and stores the path to a certain Web site. Creating bookmarks enables a quick return to favorite sites.

browser A graphic interface program that helps manage the process of locating information on the World Wide Web. Browser programs such as Netscape Navigator and Microsoft Internet Explorer provide simple searching techniques and create paths that can return you to sites you visited previously.

chat (Internet Relay Chat) A live "talk" session with other Internet or network users in which a conversation is exchanged back and forth.

client program A computer program designed to talk to a specific server program. The FTP client program is designed to ask for and use the FTP service offered by an FTP server program. Client programs usually run in your own computer, and talk to server programs in the computers it connects to.

client A computer that is signing onto another computer. The computer that is logging on acts as the client; the other computer acts as the server.

complex search Uses two or more words in a text string (and may also use operators that modify the search string) to search for matches in a search engine's catalog.

compressed file A file that has been made smaller (without lost data) by using a file compression program such as pkzip or StuffIt. Compressed files are easier to send across the Internet, as they take less time to upload and download.

copyright The legal right of ownership of published material. E-mail messages are covered by copyright laws. In most cases, the copyright owner is the writer of the message.

crawlers Another name for search engines.

directories Also referred to as folders. Directories are lists of files and other directories. They are used for organizing and storing computer files.

domain The portion of an Internet address that follows the @ symbol and identifies the computer you are logging onto.

downloading Copying files (e-mail, software, documents, etc.) from a remote computer to your own computer.

e-mail (electronic mail) A communication system for exchanging messages and attached files. E-mail can be sent to anyone in the world as long as both parties have access to the Internet and an Internet address to identify them.

Glossary

encoding A method of converting a binary file to ASCII format for e-mail purposes. Common encoding schemes include Uuencoding and MIME (Base64) encoding.

fair use The right to use short quotes and excerpts from copyrighted material such as e-mail messages.

FAQ (Frequently Asked Questions document) A text document that contains a collection of frequently asked questions about a particular subject. FAQs on many subjects are commonly available on the Web.

file "File" is a general term usually used to describe a computer document. It may also be used to refer to more than one file, however, such as groups of documents, software, games, etc.

folders/ directories Folders, also referred to as directories, are organized storage areas for maintaining computer files. Like filing cabinets, they help you manage your documents and files.

font A typeface that contains particular style and size specifications.

freeware Software that can be used for free forever. No license is required and the software may be copied and distributed legally.

FTP (File Transfer Protocol) The method of remotely transferring files from one computer to another over a network (or across the Internet). It requires that both the client and server computers use special communication software to talk to one another.

FTP site An Internet site that uses File Transfer Protocol and enables files to be downloaded and/or uploaded. When you access an FTP site through a browser application, however, your log-in is considered "anonymous" and will not allow uploading.

FTP (File Transfer Protocol) A computer program used to move files from one computer to another. The FTP program usually comes in two parts: a server program that runs in the computers offering the FTP service, and a client program running in computers, like yours, that wish to use the service.

Gopher A menu system that allows you to search various sources available on the Internet. It is a browsing system that works much like a directory or folder. Each entry may contain files and/or more directories to dig through.

heading fields (headings) Individual fields, like To and From, in the header of an e-mail message.

hierarchically structured catalog A catalog of Web sites that is organized into a few major categories that have sub-categories under them. Each sub-category has additional sub-categories under it. The level of detail in this structure depends on the particular Web site.

home page A Web site's starting point. A home page is like a table of contents. It outlines what a particular site has to offer, and usually contains connecting links to other related areas of the Internet as well.

host A central computer that other computers log onto for the purpose of sharing and exchanging information.

hot lists Lists of Web sites that you have visited or "ear-marked" and wish to return to later. Your browser program will store the paths to those sites and generate a short-cut list for future reference.

HTML (HyperText Mark Up Language) The programming language used to create Web pages so that they can be viewed, read, and accessed from any computer running on any type of operating system.

HTTP (HyperText Transfer Protocol) The communication protocol that allows for Web pages to connect to one another, regardless of what type of operating system is used to display or access the files.

hypertext or hypermedia The system of developing clickable text and objects (pictures, sound, video, etc.) to create links to related documents or different sites on the Internet.

inbox Where incoming e-mail messages are stored and retrieved.

Information Superhighway Nickname for the Internet: a vast highway by which countless pieces of information are made available and exchanged back and forth among its many users.

Internet A worldwide computer network that connects several thousand businesses, schools, research foundations, individuals, and other networks. Anyone with access can log on, communicate via e-mail, and search for various types of information.

Internet address The user ID utilized by an individual or host computer on the Internet. An Internet address is usually associated with the ID used to send and receive e-mail. It consists of the user's ID followed by the domain.

Internet Protocol The method of communication which allows information to be exchanged across the Internet and across varying platforms that may be accessing or sending information.

ISP (Internet Service Providers) Private or public organizations that offer access to the Internet. Most charge a monthly or annual fee and generally offer such features as e-mail accounts, a pre-determined number of hours for Internet access time (or unlimited access for a higher rate), special interest groups, etc.

links Hypertext or hypermedia objects that, once selected, will connect you to related documents or other areas of interest.

login A process by which you gain access to a computer by giving it your username and password. If the computer doesn't recognize your login, access will be denied.

macro virus A virus written in the macro language of a particular program (such as Word) and contained in a program document. When the document is opened, the macro is executed, and the virus usually adds itself to other, similar documents. Macro virus can be only as destructive as the macro language allows.

message header The group of heading fields at the start of every e-mail program, used by the e-mail system to route and otherwise deal with your mail.

meta-tree structured catalog Another term for hierarchically structured catalog.

modem A piece of equipment (either internal or external) that allows a computer to connect to a phone line for the purpose of dialing into the Internet, another network, or an individual computer.

modem speed (baud rate) Indicates at what speed your computer will be able to communicate with a computer on the other end. The higher the rate, the quicker the response time for accessing files and Web pages, processing images, downloading software, etc.

multimedia The process of using various computer formats: pictures, text, sound, movies, etc.

multithread search engines Software that searches the Web sites of other search engines and gathers the results of these searches for your use.

netiquette (Network etiquette) The network equivalent of respectfulness and civility in dealing with people and organizations.

network A group of computers (two or more) that are connected to one another through various means, usually cable or dial-in connections.

newsgroup A bulletin board of news information. Users specify which news topic they are interested in, and subscribe to receive information on that topic.

newsreader A program that allows you to read and respond to Usenet newsgroups.

offline The process of performing certain tasks, such as preparing e-mail messages, prior to logging onto the Internet.

online The process of performing certain tasks, such as searching the Web or responding to e-mail, while actually logged onto the Internet.

online services Organizations that usually offer Internet access as well as other services, such as shareware, technical support, group discussions, and more. Most online services charge a monthly or annual fee.

operators Words or symbols that modify the search string instead of being part of it.

outbox Where offline e-mail messages are stored. The contents of an outbox are uploaded to the Internet once you log on and prompt your e-mail program to send them.

packet A body of information that is passed through the Internet. It contains the sender's and receiver's addresses and the item that is being sent. Internet Protocol is used to route and process the packet.

platform Refers to the type of computer and its corresponding operating system, such as PC, Macintosh, UNIX. The Internet is a multi-platform entity, meaning that all types of computers can access it.

POP (Post Office Protocol) The method used to transfer e-mail messages from your mail server to your system.

public domain freeware Software that can be used for free; usually the author is anonymous.

quote format A way of displaying text quoted from other e-mail messages, most frequently used in replies. Quoted text usually has a character like ">" at the start of each line. Some e-mail programs let you set the style of quoted material.

search engine A software program that goes out on the Web, seeks Web sites, and catalogs them – usually by downloading their home pages.

search sites Web sites that contain catalogs of Web resources that can be searched by headings, URLs, and key words.

self-extracting archive Macintosh-platform compressed file that does not require external software for decompression. These files usually end with an .sea extension.

self-extracting file PC-platform compressed file that does not require external software for decompression. These files usually end with an .exe extension.

server program A computer program that offers a service to other computer programs called client programs. The FTP server program offers the FTP service to FTP client programs. Server programs usually run in computers you will be connecting to.

server A computer that is accessed by other computers on a network. It usually shares files with or provides other services to the client computers that log onto it.

shareware Computer programs, utilities and other items (fonts, games, etc.) that can be downloaded or distributed free of charge, but with the understanding that if you wish to continue using it, you will send the suggested fee to the developer.

signature A few lines of text automatically appended to the body of an e-mail message. Signatures usually include the sender's address plus other information.

simple search Uses a text string, usually a single word, to search for matches in a search engine's catalog.

.sit file A Macintosh file compressed by using a compression application called StuffIt.

SLIP (Serial Line Internet Protocol) Software that allows for a direct serial connection to the Internet. SLIP allows your computer to become part of the Internet – not just a terminal accessing the Internet. If your computer is set up with SLIP, you can Telnet or FTP other computers directly without having to go through an Internet provider.

SMTP (Simple Mail Transfer Protocol) The method used to transfer e-mail messages between servers and from your system to your mail server.

spiders Another name for search engines.

standalone FTP client program A standalone computer program designed to talk to an FTP server program running at a remote computer site that offers FTP services. The FTP client program can ask for the files you want and send files you wish to deliver. The client program runs in your computer; the server program runs at the site.

start page The opening page within a browser application. This is the page from which all other Web site links are built. A browser's start page is its home page by default, but you can customize your browser to begin with any Web site as your start page.

subject-structured catalog A catalog organized under a few broad subject headings. The number and names of these headings depend on the Web site.

surfing the Internet Exploring various World Wide Web sites and links to search for information on the Internet. Using FTP, WAIS, and Gopher servers can further assist in the surfing/searching process – as can a good Internet browser.

TCP/IP (Transmission Control Protocol/ Internet Protocol) The communication system that is used between networks on the Internet. It checks to make sure that information is being correctly sent and received from one computer to another.

Telnet A program that allows one computer to log on to another host computer. This process allows you to use any of the features available on the host computer, including sharing data and software, participating in interactive discussions, etc.

text format file Same as the ASCII format file: a document that has been formatted to be read by almost any computer or program in the world.

text string A string of ASCII characters. The text string may or may not contain operators.

threaded messages Messages grouped so that replies to a message are grouped with the original message. When threaded messages are sorted, threads are kept together.

uploading The process of copying computer files (e-mail, software, documents, etc.) from one's own computer to a remote computer.

URL (Uniform Resource Locator) A locator command used only within the World Wide Web system to create or hunt for linked sites. It operates and looks much like an Internet Address.

Usenet A worldwide discussion system, operating on linked Usenet servers, consisting of a set of newsgroups where articles or messages are posted covering a variety of subjects and interests. You can use your browser or a newsreader program to access the newsgroups available from your Internet provider's Usenet server.

UUencoding One of the encoding schemes, short for UNIX-to-UNIX encoding. UUencoding is common on all platforms, not just UNIX.

virus A small, usually destructive computer program that hides inside innocent looking programs. Once the virus is executed, it attaches itself to other programs. When triggered, often by the occurrence of a date or time on the computer's internal clock/calendar, it executes a nuisance or damaging function, such as printing a message or reformatting your hard disk.

WAIS (Wide Area Information Servers) A system that allows for searches for information based on actual contents of files, not just file titles.

Web robots Software that automatically searches the Web for new sites.

Web Site A location on the Internet that represents a particular company, organization, topic, etc. It normally contains links to more information within a site, as well as suggested links to related sites on the Internet.

World Wide Web (WWW) An easy-to-use system for finding information on the Internet through the use of hypertext or hypermedia linking. Hypertext and hypermedia consist of text and graphic objects that, when you click on them, automatically link you to different areas of a site or to related Internet sites.

zip file PC file compressed with pkzip. Zipped files usually need to be unzipped with pkunzip before they can be used.

Index

Index